The BARE BONES BIBLE® FACTS

JIM GEORGE

HARVEST HOUSE PUBLISHERS

EUGENE, OREGON

Cover by Dugan Design Group, Bloomington, Minnesota

Note: All map locations are approximate, and are not to scale.

THE BARE BONES BIBLE® FACTS
Copyright © 2009 by Jim George
Published by Harvest House Publishers
Eugene, Oregon 97402
www.harvesthousepublishers.com

Library of Congress Cataloging-in-Publication Data
George, Jim, 1943-
The Bare Bones Bible facts / Jim George.
  p. cm.
ISBN 978-0-7369-2359-0 (pbk.)
1. Bible—Dictionaries. 2. Bible—Miscellanea. I. Title.
BS440.G44 2009
220.3—dc22

                                                    2009033658

Printed in the United States of America

                09 10 11 12 13 14 15 16 17 / DP-SK / 10 9 8 7 6 5 4 3 2 1

Acknowledgments

Working on the *Bare Bones Bible*® series has been a true labor of love. It's been especially rewarding because of the encouragement I've received from Bob Hawkins, the president of Harvest House Publishers. From Day One Bob has been a positive force behind the writing of all the books in the *Bare Bones Bible*® series. This is particularly true now with this volume, *The Bare Bones Bible*® *Facts*. From the inception of this branded series, Bob has suggested a book that deals with the many interesting facts, stories, and people of the Bible. At last this book is a reality, and I offer my heartfelt thanks to Bob Hawkins for his support and interest in this project.

A special thanks must also go to Benjamin Hawkins, who was instrumental in diligently compiling much of the initial material for this book. Ben is a student of God's Word, a man who has and is continuing to seek the scholarly training that will further prepare him for a life of writing his own books and assisting others.

I also cannot thank my editor, Steve Miller, enough. Steve is a friend and a senior editor at Harvest House Publishers. I thank God for Steve, for his valuable assistance and editorial expertise during the writing of this book, and for all the other book projects we have worked on together. Steve makes writing a lot easier because of his wisdom, his understanding of God's Word, and his years of editorial experience.

Terry Glaspey, the director of acquisitions and development at Harvest House, has also been extremely helpful with his many insights and biblical and theological suggestions. All the books in this *Bare Bones Bible*® series have benefited from his greatly appreciated input.

Finally, a heartfelt thanks must go to the design and production department at Harvest House for the page layouts for all the books in the *Bare Bones Bible*® series. They have helped make all the books very appealing and readable.

Many thanks to all my friends and helpers at Harvest House Publishers.

Contents

Introduction

Have you ever wondered about some background fact while you were reading a passage of Scripture? Or, while working a lesson for a Bible study, have you ever wanted to know more about some passing bit of information?

Well, those things happen to me a lot! I love digging into the behind-the-scenes facts of what I'm reading in the Bible. And that's part of the reason I wrote this book about the facts of the Bible—facts that I, too, am curious about knowing for my own spiritual growth!

Another reason for this book is to complement the other volumes in *The Bare Bones Bible*® series—*The Bare Bone Bible*® *Handbook* and *The Bare Bone Bible*® *Bios*. When I finished writing those two books, it was suggested to me that these bare bones treatments of the *books* of the Bible and the *people* of the Bible could be supplemented by many interesting and helpful *facts* for anyone who desires to know more about the Bible.

That's why *The Bare Bones Bible*® *Facts* was written—to encourage you to expand your knowledge, understanding, and appreciation of the Bible and its message. As you glance through this book you'll notice that the topics are laid out in alphabetical order from A to Z. This will allow you to use the book as a "quick reference" while you're reading and studying your Bible. And, because of the many "Life Lessons" and "Did you know…?" features throughout the book, you can also read it like an inspirational devotional. Either way, like reading your Bible, there's no wrong way to use this book.

Obviously, due to the intentionally brief treatment of each entry, some information has been omitted. This doesn't mean the excluded material is unimportant. It just means that when you want to dig deeper on a given topic, you'll want to refer to more comprehensive works. Your desire to know more will fulfill my goal for you and me—the goal of getting more involved in understanding the Bible and God's many messages to us.

I'm praying for your growth in God's grace and in knowledge,

Jim George

The Bare Bones Bible®
Facts from A to Z

A

Aaron

Meet Aaron, the brother of Moses and the first high priest of Israel. God had Aaron serve as Moses' spokesman because Moses claimed he was slow of speech. Unfortunately, Aaron's behavior did not always honor God. In one instance, while Moses was receiving the Ten Commandments—one of which was to have no other gods before God—the people urged Aaron to make a god to worship.

What did Aaron do? He gave in. He collected gold from the people and made a golden calf. His excuse to Moses was that he couldn't resist the people's pressure. He claimed he took the gold from them, threw it into the fire, and out came a calf! Later, Aaron failed again when God told him and Moses to speak to a rock and water would flow from it. Moses, with apparent approval from Aaron, struck the rock instead of speaking to it. Because of this act of disobedience, Aaron died at Mt. Hor without entering the land of Canaan—the Promised Land.

No leader is perfect, but for the most part Aaron followed God and served Him by using the skills and abilities God gave him.[1]

A Life Lesson from Aaron

Living in the Shadow

According to the custom of the day, Aaron, as the older brother, should have been the leader of Israel instead of his younger brother, Moses. But God chose Moses instead. The result? Aaron spent the rest of his days in the shadow of his younger brother. Aaron had his shortcomings, yet he shines as an example of a strong team player, co-laborer, and assistant to the person God designated as the leader of His people. Are you a team player in the ministry of your church? Can you allow others to lead while you follow with a servant's heart? Do you delight in assisting those God has called to lead? God used both Aaron and Moses to lead His people. As He did with Aaron, God wants to use you to come alongside others to see that His work gets done.

Abel

The second son of Adam and Eve, Abel was the younger brother of Cain. When the brothers offered sacrifices to God, He was pleased with Abel's sacrifice but had no regard for Cain's offering. Out of jealously, Cain murdered Abel in cold blood. Abel died for obediently offering to God what was acceptable and lives forever as an example of righteousness and faith (Hebrews 11:4). (For Abel's story, see Genesis 4:1-8.)

A Life Lesson from Abel

Offering What Is Acceptable

Our devotion for God is measured by the offerings we bring to Him, and the attitude behind the offerings. Abel possessed a heart of faith and a deep respect for God. Therefore he gladly offered God what was pleasing and acceptable. When you give—whether it's your time, your energy, your possessions, or your money—is it with a joyful heart? Do you give because you have to or because you want to? And do you give your best? No one can outgive God, so give God what is acceptable…and give it from your heart.

Abram/Abraham

Abraham (meaning "father of a multitude") is one of the most important figures in the Bible. He was the first of the patriarchs (Abraham, Isaac, and Jacob), the father of the Israelite nation, from which came the Jewish people. Known initially as Abram ("exalted father"), God told him to leave his own country and go to another land. God promised to bless Abraham, make him a great nation, and make him a blessing to all the families of the earth. How did Abraham respond to such an order? He took his wife, Sarah (initially named Sarai), and left all that he had known to follow God into the unknown. (See Genesis 11:26–17:5; 1 Chronicles 1:27; Nehemiah 9:7.)

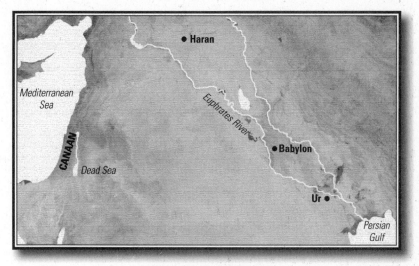

The Travels of Abraham
God called Abraham to leave Ur and go to Canaan.
En route, Abraham stayed at Haran.

God made another important promise to Abraham, which was the promise of a son from his barren wife, Sarah—a son who would produce nations, kings, and peoples. In response to God's promise, Abraham fell on his face and laughed, wondering how he and his wife—being as old as they were—could possibly have a child. For 25 years Abraham waited for the promised son. His time of waiting was a time of testing and strengthening his faith and trust in God as he aged to 100 and Sarah, well past the age of childbearing, became 90. At last, through a miracle, Isaac—meaning "laughter"—was born! God, as always, faithfully fulfilled His promise. (See Genesis 17:15-19; 21:1-7.)

In the New Testament we also read about Abraham. Jesus mentioned Abraham in one of His parables, and Paul referred to Abraham in his discussion of justification by faith apart from works. (See Luke 16:19-31; Romans 4; Galatians 3:6-9.)

A Life Lesson from Abraham

Obedience Brings Blessing

Abraham was a man who obeyed God. Abraham was told by God to leave his country and go to Palestine. He was told where to go and what to do...and he did it. What is your level of obedience to God? How compliant are you to God's commands and instructions?

If you're having a problem with doing what God asks, expects, and requires, acknowledge your weakness. Act to exercise and strengthen the muscle of obedience in the little things. Then, when some seemingly impossible challenge comes along, you can respond like Abraham. You can quickly, quietly, and without question obey God.

God's blessing awaited Abraham on the other side of every act of obedience. And the same is true for you. Don't miss out on God's blessings by not following and obeying Him.

Adam

Adam was the first man. God formed Adam (from the Hebrew word *adam*, meaning "mankind") from the dust of the ground and put him in the Garden of Eden to tend and keep it. God also put trees in the garden—including the tree of life, and the tree of the knowledge of good and evil. He then told Adam he could eat freely from every tree of the garden *except* the tree of the knowledge of good and evil. He explained to Adam that if or when he ate of that tree, on that day he would die.

After Adam and Eve disobeyed God and ate from the forbidden tree, God came to the rescue and salvaged their lives. He covered their sin by killing animals to make clothes for them. He sent them out of the garden so they wouldn't eat of the tree of life and experience perpetual death. He also pointed to a glorious future—a Savior who would help them (Genesis 3:15).

Adam's sin of disobeying God spread sin to all mankind (Romans 5:12). After Adam was expelled from Eden, he and his wife, Eve, had two sons named Cain and Abel, and at least one other child, a son they named Seth. Adam died when he was 930 years old. (See Genesis 2:15–5:5.)

The Named Sons of Adam and Eve

Cain, meaning "to acquire" or "to get," was the first murderer.

Abel, meaning "fleeting breath" or "vapor," was the first person to die.

Seth, meaning "restitution," replaced Abel in the godly line of Messiah.

Adam had other sons and daughters, but their names are not revealed to us (Genesis 5:4).

A Life Lesson from Adam

A Picture of God's Grace

The life of Adam gives us a glimpse of what God originally intended for mankind—a perfect relationship with Him in a perfect environment of health and peace. It also paints a picture of the disastrous effects of disobeying God. But, as if we were viewing scenes in a slide show, we are treated to a display of God's grace and hope: In His mercy, God stepped in and saved the day, spared Adam and Eve, and secured a future for His fallen people.

Are you experiencing God's grace through the "last Adam," Jesus Christ (1 Corinthians 15:45)? If so, you are presently living in a perfect relationship with God that will one day be permanently realized in heaven—that perfect place where, once again, all things will be perfect.

Altar

An altar is a raised structure or place on which sacrifices are offered or incense is burned in worship. Throughout history, nations have built elaborate structures to offer sacrifices to their gods. Coming out of Egypt, the children of Israel were very familiar with pagan worship. In order not to pervert their worship of the one true God, Moses was immediately instructed while on Mount Sinai to build two altars:

- the altar of burnt offering (also called the bronze altar or the table of the Lord), upon which the morning and evening sacrifices were offered, and

- the altar of incense (also called the golden altar, which stood in the holy place of the tabernacle) upon which sweet spices were continually burned. The morning and evening services were commenced by the high priest offering incense on this altar.

Later, God allowed other altars to be used in places other than the tabernacle and later, the temple.[2]

Angel

The English term *angel* (from the Greek *angelos*) means "messenger." Essentially, in Scripture, an angel is a messenger from God.

The Bible speaks of both good and bad angels. The most well-known bad angel is Lucifer, whose pride caused him to fall from heaven. He became known as Satan and the Devil. Other bad angels are referred to as demons and devils. Some of the well-known good angels are Michael ("the archangel") and Gabriel.

As messengers, angels announced and heralded the birth of Christ. They also tended to Jesus Christ in the wilderness and in the garden of Gethsemane. They were present at the empty tomb of the resurrected Lord and at His ascension into heaven.[3]

Angel of the Lord

The angel of the Lord was a theophany, a self-manifestation of God to men. This particular angel is distinguished in Scripture from all others and is identified by several names, including...

- "the Angel of the LORD"
- "the angel of God"
- "the Angel of His Presence"

He is clearly identified with the Lord Himself in His self-manifestation to men. (See Genesis 16:7; 21:17; 31:11-13; Judges 2:1; Isaiah 63:9.)

Appearances of the Angel of the Lord to Old Testament People

Hagar—received encouragement and instruction (Genesis 16:7; 21:17)

Abraham—received a visit and a promise (Genesis 18)

Moses—received his call to lead God's people (Exodus 3:2)

Balaam—was told to take a message to King Balak (Numbers 22:35)

Israelites—were given a message describing their disobedience (Judges 2)

Gideon—was called a mighty hero (Judges 6:11)

Manoah's wife—was promised a son (Judges 13:3)

Manoah—was reassured of the promised son (Judges 13:11)

Elijah—was encouraged and strengthened to continue his journey (1 Kings 19:7)

Animals of the Bible

The Bible is filled with references to animals. A sampling of the many animals mentioned in Scripture includes:

Bear. Bears were fearsome animals in the ancient Near East because of their strength, size, and unpredictable nature. In fact, when a group of young men made fun of the prophet Elisha's baldness, two bears came out of the woods and mauled 42 of them (2 Kings 2:23-24). David, the shepherd boy (and later the king of Israel), developed the skills necessary to defend his sheep from a lion and a bear. This skill possibly impressed King Saul enough that he let the young David fight the giant Goliath (1 Samuel 17:33-37).

Behemoth. There is much debate as to the identity of the "behemoth" mentioned in Job 40:15-24. Grammatically, it probably means "super beast." What exactly was this super beast? Some think it was a hippopotamus. Others say it must have been a crocodile because a hippo doesn't have a tail that swings like a cedar. Still others have suggested that it was a dinosaur. No one is sure.

Camel. These gangly creatures were typically used as beasts of burden. Camels have always been ideal for desert travel because of their ability to conserve water in their humps. There are two types of Middle Eastern camels—those with one hump and those with two humps. Their hides were also used for coverings. Both Elijah and John the Baptist were clothed in camel's hair. Jesus referred to camels when illustrating His sermons, pointing out the absurdities of a camel passing through the eye of a needle and of a person attempting to swallow a camel. (See 2 Kings 1:8; Matthew 3:4; Matthew 19:24; 23:24.)

Donkey. Like camels, donkeys were used for travel in Bible times. Donkeys were considered a financial asset, for to own many donkeys and camels was considered a sign of great wealth.

In a delightful story, God gave the donkey who was carrying the false prophet, Balaam, a voice and enabled the animal to "see" the angel of the Lord (while the prophet did not) and to talk to the prophet. (Equally amazing is the fact that Balaam talked back to the donkey!) And more than 500 years before the birth of Christ, the Old Testament prophet Zechariah announced that the Messiah would come on a colt, the foal of a donkey. Jesus fulfilled this prophecy when He rode into Jerusalem on a donkey at the beginning of the week before His crucifixion. (See Numbers 22:22-31; Zechariah 9:9; Matthew 21:1-11.)

Leviathan. The Bible describes Leviathan as a twisted serpent, a reptile in the sea whom God will punish, and a terrible beast whom no one but God can defeat. Scripture says that God easily crushes Leviathan's heads. Essentially, Leviathan is God's toy—this mighty, chaotic beast succumbs to the infinitely greater power of the King of kings.

What was Leviathan? An ancient dinosaur? A killer whale? A great white shark? Whatever it was, it is presented in the Bible as the ultimate killer beast, more fearsome than all the other sea creatures. And whatever it was, man was its toy. But this beast was no match for God. (See Isaiah 27:1; Job 41; Psalm 74:14; 104:26.)

Lion. Lions were powerful foes in the ancient world, and in the Middle East, they were considered royalty. The patriarch Jacob blessed his son Judah and compared him to a lion, saying that the scepter would not depart from his descendants. Scripture later refers to Jesus as "the Lion of the tribe of Judah." (See Genesis 49:9; Revelation 5:5.)

Sheep. Sheep were extremely important animals to the people of Bible times; they were a form of wealth. Their hide and wool were used as clothing, and they provided food for people. Sheep were also used for sacrifices to God.

At the first Passover, while the Israelites were still in Egypt, lamb's blood was sprinkled on the doorposts of each dwelling to keep the

angel of death from killing the firstborn of that house.

In the New Testament, John the Baptist called Jesus "the Lamb of God," the ultimate sacrifice whose death would take away the sin of the world. (See Exodus 12; Isaiah 53:7; John 1:29.)

Snake. Because many snakes in the Middle East are poisonous, it's not hard to imagine why snakes are often seen as dangerous, crafty, and evil, creatures to be avoided at all costs. The Hebrew term for a snake (*nachash*) was probably derived from the sound of a serpent's hiss.

It was a serpent who tempted Eve to commit the first-ever sin on earth. That serpent was more cunning than any beast of the field which God had made. The patriarch Jacob, in a very uncomplimentary prophecy, compared his son Dan to "a viper by the path, that bites the horse's heels" so its rider is thrown off (Genesis 49:17).

Snake—or *viper* or *serpent*—is definitely not a positive term. John the Baptist called the religious leaders of Israel a brood of vipers, and the devil is referred to as the old serpent. (See Genesis 3:1; 49:17; Matthew 3:7; Revelation 12:9.)

A Life Lesson from Sheep

One of God's Sheep

The Bible often refers to humans as sheep. But don't get too excited. This isn't a compliment! Sheep, generally known to be dumb animals, lack careful thinking and initiative. They are lazy, can easily be led astray, and frequently wander into danger. According to Isaiah 53:6, we are like sheep who fail to follow, who go our own way and do our own thing. The bad news is, this is our nature. But the good news is that God sent His Son Jesus to lead us and take care of us. He is the Good Shepherd who knows His sheep and calls them by name. He gave His life for those who believe in Him. (See John 10:7-18.)

Read through Psalm 23. Be sure and notice all that the Lord, the Good Shepherd, does and will do for you as His sheep. He truly can take care of your every need...if you follow Him. How closely are you following Him today?

Psalm 23

The LORD is my shepherd;
I shall not want.
He makes me to lie down in green pastures;
He leads me beside the still waters.

He restores my soul;
He leads me in the paths of righteousness
For His name's sake.

Yea, though I walk through the valley of the shadow of death,
I will fear no evil;
For You are with me;
Your rod and Your staff, they comfort me.

You prepare a table before me in the presence of my enemies;
You anoint my head with oil;
My cup runs over.
Surely goodness and mercy shall follow me
All the days of my life;
And I will dwell in the house of the LORD forever.

Anointed One

The expectation of *the* Anointed One—the Messiah—is found throughout the Hebrew Scriptures. The term *Messiah* (Hebrew=*mashiach*, which means "anointed one") appears in the Old Testament in Daniel 9:25-26. Many Old Testament prophets spoke of someone who would be born into this world, bring peace, rule all Israel, and save the people of Israel and the rest of the world from their sins. In fact, many interpreters have seen this as far back as Genesis 3:15, believing that verse to be a prophecy of the Messiah, the Anointed One. In the New Testament, the Greek word *christos*—Christ—is a translation of the Hebrew *mashiach*, or Messiah. As we now know, Jesus was the Christ, the Messiah, the Anointed One. (See Daniel 9:25-26; Isaiah 7:14; 9:6; Isaiah 2; 11; 53; Micah 5:2.)

Some People and Objects Anointed in Scripture

High Priests—Exodus 29:7,29

Priests—Exodus 28:41

Saul—in 1 Samuel 9:16

David—1 Samuel 16:3,12

Solomon—1 Kings 1:39

Jehu—1 Kings 19:16

Hazael—1 Kings 19:15

Joash—2 Kings 11:12

Jehoahaz—2 Kings 23:30

Cyrus—referred to as anointed in Isaiah 45:1

Prophets—1 Kings 19:16

The tabernacle—Exodus 30:26

The altar in the tabernacle—Exodus 30:26-28

The vessels in the tabernacle—Exodus 30:27-28

Anointment

To anoint someone in Bible times was to take a flask of oil and pour it on him. Usually this was done to designate the person as set apart and consecrated by God for a holy purpose.

The Bible speaks of many "anointed" ones. The sons of Aaron were anointed priests. Samuel anointed Saul and David when they were appointed kings over Israel. Also, when David was running from Saul, he recognized Saul's status as king and refused to kill him because Saul was "the LORD's anointed." Because he was used by God, King Cyrus of Persia was also called God's "anointed." (See Numbers 3:3; 1 Samuel 10:1; 16:13; 24:6,10; 26:9,11-23; Isaiah 45:1.)

Antichrist

The Greek term *antichristos* means "against Christ," and the Antichrist is described as the "man of lawlessness" (NASB) who will come and desecrate the temple in the last days and declare himself God. Many biblical commentators have applied this term to the beast who rises from the sea in Revelation 13. During the end times, this beast will win the devotion and worship of people throughout the world. He will also control the global economy. Ultimately, however, Christ will conquer the beast—the Antichrist—and send him into the lake of fire. (See Daniel 7:20-21; 9:26-27; 2 Thessalonians 2:1-12; 1 John 2:18,22; 4:3; 2 John 7; Revelation 13:16-17; 19:20).

Apostle

An apostle (Greek=*apostolos*) was one who was sent. In the context of Christianity, this was one who was sent in a special way by Jesus to preach the good news. The term first appears when the 12 disciples were initially sent by Jesus to preach that the kingdom of heaven was at hand. The apostles were described as the foundation of the church, the body of Christ. Paul also considered himself an apostle of Christ Jesus and pointed out that men did not send him to preach the gospel—it was Jesus Himself. (See Matthew 10:2-5; Ephesians 1:1; 2:20; Galatians 1:1; Acts 9.)

Those Who Bear the Title *Apostle* in the New Testament

The Original 12

    Simon, also called Peter

    Andrew, Peter's brother

    James, the son of Zebedee

    John, James' brother and the son of Zebedee

Philip, the one who asked how Jesus would feed the 5000

Bartholomew, also known as Nathanael

Thomas, also known as the twin and one who doubted

Matthew, the tax collector

James, the son of Alphaeus

Thaddaeus, also known as Judas, the son of James

Simon, the Zealot

Judas Iscariot, who later betrayed Jesus

Others Who Were Called or Considered Apostles

Matthias, chosen later to take Judas' place

Saul, named Paul, chosen by Jesus to preach to Gentiles

Barnabas, Titus, Epaphroditus, and other missionaries

(See Matthew 10:1-4; Acts 1:26; Romans 1:1.)

A Life Lesson from the Apostles

Messengers of the Good News

Here's something to think about: The first group of "good news messengers" were ordained by Jesus and called apostles. Their ministry ceased with the death of John, the last surviving apostle. The second group of messengers was made up of ordinary people—men like Barnabas, Titus, Epaphroditus, and others—who faithfully shared the gospel.

Who are God's messengers today? You are, if you are following in the footsteps of these groups and taking the message of Jesus Christ next door, around the block, to the workplace, and to the ends of the earth. Recall how you first heard the good news of the gospel of Christ. Whom did God "send" to you with the message of salvation? Now, whom do you know who needs to hear the good news from you?

Ararat, Mount

No one can dogmatically point to a precise location for a singular Mount Ararat. The mountains of Ararat are a craggy, rugged range of mountains in modern-day Armenia. The Bible says Noah's ark settled on a mountain in the "mountains of Ararat" when the floodwaters began to subside. For this reason, much speculation and several expeditions have stimulated interest in this remote area. But in general the term *Mount Ararat* is applied to a high and almost inaccessible mountain that rises majestically from the plain below. It has two peaks, about seven miles apart—one is 14,300 feet and the other is 10,300 feet above the level of the plain. The top 3000 feet of the higher peak is perpetually covered with snow. It is called Kuh-i-nuh ("Noah's mountain") by the Persians. Most of the searching for evidence of Noah's ark is concentrated there today. (See Genesis 8:4.)

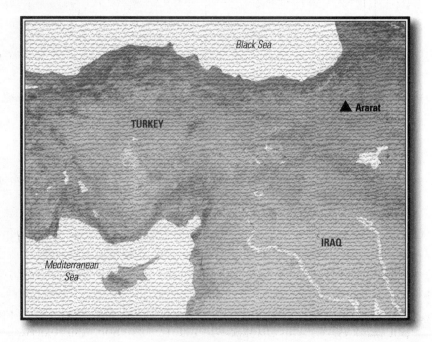

Mount Ararat

Ark of the Covenant

The Ark of the Covenant was built by the people of Israel under God's instruction and placed in the Holy of Holies in the tabernacle (and later, in Solomon's temple). It was made of acacia wood and was about three feet nine inches long, two feet three inches wide, and two feet three inches high. Four gold rings—two on each end—were fastened to it. Two poles were inserted through the rings—one pole on each side—so the ark could be lifted and moved. On  the lid of the ark was the mercy seat, made of pure gold. On each side of the mercy seat were two golden cherubim facing one another with their wings outstretched. The two tablets with the Ten Commandments on them were kept inside the ark. Aaron's budded rod and a gold jar with manna in it were also inside the ark.

Once a year the high priest entered the Holy of Holies to make atonement for the whole nation of Israel. If he or anyone else entered at any other time, they would die. The ark was to be treated with great reverence because it depicted God's presence. Those who mishandled the Ark of the Covenant became sick or died. (See Exodus 25:10-22; 1 Kings 8:6-9; Hebrews 9:4,7; 2 Samuel 6:7.)

A Life Lesson from the Ark of the Covenant

Come Before God with Confidence

Take a minute and try to picture this: Situated in the Holy of Holies, the glory of God resided above the Ark of the Covenant. Only one person—the high priest—could enter this most sacred place, and only once a year, to sprinkle blood upon the mercy seat to atone for the sins of the people. This is a fearsome and scary scene! But thank God all this changed when He sent His Son, Jesus Christ. As the perfect and therefore the permanent sacrifice for sin, Jesus atoned for the sins of all who put their faith and trust in Him. As a result...

- You and all believers today have free access to God...all the time.

- You are blessed to live in God's constant presence, knowing He is always with you.

- You can go boldly before God at any time, without fear and with full confidence.

- You can approach God and receive His mercy when you fail.

- You can find spiritual strength and grace anytime you need it (Hebrews 4:16).

Come before Him now. Give thanks for the freedom you enjoy as you worship and walk with Him, a freedom Jesus Christ secured for you at a high cost.

Ark of Noah

God told Noah to build a ship (Hebrew=*tevah,* which means "ark" or "box") to protect him, his family, and two of every kind of animal from the world's first-ever and largest-ever flood. The ark was commissioned by God to preserve Noah and his family and one male-female set of each species of animals for a yearlong boat ride. What size "boat" was needed to house more than 100,000 animals and their food...for a year? This oblong floating house was made of gopherwood, covered with pitch, and was

- 450 feet long,
- 75 feet wide,
- 45 feet high with
- 3 levels, each 15 feet high.

The ark had a door on the side and a window on the roof. That was some kind of boat—so awesome and complex that it took Noah 120 years to build. (See Genesis 6:1-22.)

A Life Lesson from Noah's Ark

How Big Is Your Faith?

Noah was commanded to build a gigantic boat—a boat the size of one-and-a-half football fields—for a phenomenon that had yet to occur since the creation of the world: rain. Yet Noah obeyed. Can you imagine the faith Noah exhibited as he worked on this project... for 120 years?!

Faith is described in the Bible as the assurance of things hoped for and a conviction of things we cannot see (Hebrews 11:1). Faith is trust. Noah trusted God to do what He said He would do in the future. And Noah believed in something no human had ever seen or heard of before. Therefore Noah carried out God's instructions.

How big is your faith? If it's small and faltering, start with small steps of trusting obedience. Then when something big comes along—like spending a lifetime building the world's largest lifeboat—you, like Noah, will be ready to start hammering away!

Did you know...?

The average size of land animals is less than the size of a sheep. Some 18,000 species are alive today, and even when that number is doubled, the ark was more than big enough to carry them all. It had the capacity to hold more than 100,000 animals the size of a sheep. The ark definitely had ample room for all the animals, fowl, reptiles, and insects, as well as food for all the creatures and Noah and his family for one year!

Armor of God

Christians are exhorted to put on specific pieces of armor or spiritual clothing provided by God as protection for the lifelong, daily battle against the devil and sin. (See Ephesians 6:11-17.)

- ▶ The waistband/belt of truth
- ▶ The breastplate/body armor of righteousness
- ▶ The shoes of the gospel of peace
- ▶ The shield of faith
- ▶ The helmet of salvation
- ▶ The sword of the Spirit

Checklist for Spiritual Victory

What can you do to equip yourself and prepare for battle today... and every day?

- ✓ Don't underestimate the power of your enemy, Satan.
- ✓ Don't neglect to put on the armor God provides.
- ✓ Don't forget to pray to stand strong in the power of God's might.
- ✓ Don't forget you are in a spiritual battle every minute of every day.

> "Put on the whole armor of God,
> that you may be able to stand against the wiles of the devil"
>
> (EPHESIANS 6:11).

Assyria

The Assyrians were the offspring of Asshur, a son of Shem (who was a son of Noah). The country of Assyria was located east of the Tigris River, and its capital was Nineveh. In 738 B.C., the Assyrians invaded Israel (the northern kingdom). The Assyrians were on their way to becoming a world power while the surrounding countries—Syria, Israel, and Judah—were declining.

In 722 B.C. the Assyrians took all the people of Samaria and the kingdom of Israel into captivity. They continued to build their empire until Nineveh—the powerful capital city—was sacked by the Babylonians in 612 B.C. (See Genesis 10:22; 2 Kings 15:19; 17–18.)

Augustus (Caesar)

Augustus (also known as Octavius) was born in 63 B.C. He was the grandnephew of Julius Caesar and was adopted as the son of Julius Caesar. He became the first Roman emperor when he won the battle of Actium in 31 B.C. Palestine was under his rule when Jesus Christ was born. Because Caesar Augustus issued a decree that all citizens of the empire had to return to their cities of birth for a census, Jesus ended up being born in Bethlehem instead of his parents' hometown of Nazareth. This fulfilled a prophecy God had foretold 500 years earlier through the prophet Micah.

Roman rulers were considered gods. And yet the tiny baby born in an animal stall in a town under the rule of this "god" was the true God, God in flesh, the One who would rule all heaven and earth. Augustus died in A.D. 14; Jesus lives forever. (See Luke 2:1; Micah 5:2).

B

Baal

Baal was the most popular god in Canaan, where God had sent His people to settle and inhabit. Baal was an idol made into the form of a bull, the symbol of strength and fertility. He was the god of the sun, and the god of the rains and harvest. Baal worship also included prostitution.

The Israelites faced the temptation of Baal worship on a daily basis. Time and time again they failed, and God had to chasten His people to bring them back to Himself. The most famous confrontation between Baal worship and the worship of God came when Elijah, the prophet, challenged the priests of Baal to offer sacrifices to determine who was the one true God. The 450 prophets of Baal could not pass the test, so Elijah killed them. (See 1 Kings 18:25-40.)

Babel, Tower of

The famous story of the Tower of Babel began when there was one language spoken by all the people on the whole earth. Some of the people journeyed east and settled in the land of Shinar. There they decided to build a tall tower that would give them a reputation for greatness. They believed this tower would keep them from being scattered throughout the earth. The tower was probably a ziggurat—an ancient Mesopotamian structure. Such buildings were generally pyramid shaped and about 300 feet high and wide, imposing edifices that could be seen from far distances. But God intervened by confusing their language, which caused the people to scatter all over the earth. As a result, the city they were building was called "Babel" (Babylon) because God "confused" (Hebrew=*balal*) their language. (See Genesis 11:1-9.)

Babylon

Babylon was both an evil city and an immoral empire. It was a world center for idol worship. Three times this mighty nation invaded Judah and took captives back to Babylon with them. (Daniel and his friends Shadrach, Meshach, and Abed-nego were youths who were carried away during one of the deportations to Babylon.)

Babylon's riches came from the misfortunes of others. The prophet Isaiah predicted its destruction about 200 years before Babylon became part of the Persian empire in 539 B.C., when Cyrus invaded and conquered the land. Because Babylon was the birthplace of idolatry, in the New Testament it symbolized those who opposed God. (See Isaiah 13; Revelation 14:8.)

Baptism

In ancient Judaism, ceremonial washings served as a purification process for removing impurities from a Jew. By Jesus' day, there was a one-time-only washing that signified that a Gentile had become a Jew. But John the Baptist's baptism was for *both* Jews and Gentiles. John explained that his baptism was not the ultimate baptism. He baptized with water unto repentance, but Jesus, who was coming after John, would be mightier than John. John told the people Jesus would baptize them with the Holy Spirit and fire, not merely water (Matthew 3:11).

John's baptism—or water baptism—cannot save a person. It only serves as a public declaration of a person's faith in Jesus and commitment to walk with Him. Salvation comes when a person places faith in Jesus and His sacrificial death and resurrection.

A Life Lesson from Baptism

Baptism Is a Sign of Faith

Baptism is one of only two ordinances in the Christian church today, the other being the Lord's Supper or communion. Baptism was commanded by the Lord Himself in Matthew 28:19. It was practiced throughout the book of Acts and explained in the New Testament epistles, and is accompanied by a profession of faith. If for no other reason, the command of our Lord is sufficient justification for a believer to be baptized. In the early church, there was no such thing as an unbaptized believer.

Baptism is a symbolic and beautiful outward expression of an inward belief. Have you made your belief in Christ known to others in this public way?

Barabbas

One Jewish custom during Bible times was the release of a prisoner on Passover so he could go free. Locked away in a cell in Jerusalem in A.D. 30 was a violent revolutionary, robber, and murderer named Barabbas. After Jesus was arrested in the Garden of Gethsemane, the Roman governor Pontius Pilate asked the Passover crowd whether they wanted Barabbas or Jesus to go free. Pilate, who believed Jesus to be innocent, was astounded when the crowd chose to let Barabbas go free and urged that Jesus be crucified. In an effort to please the crowd, Pilate released Barabbas and gave them Jesus, the spotless, sinless Son of God, to be crucified. (For Barabbas' story, see Matthew 27:15-26.)

A Life Lesson from Barabbas

Free Through the Blood of Jesus

Barabbas was a sinner—a hardened sinner. He had stolen and he had killed. There was no doubt of his guilt or that he was worthy and deserving of death. Yet Jesus, the perfect and sinless Lamb of God, was executed in Barabbas' place, while Barabbas was declared to be free, absolved of all wrong. Sound familiar? The Bible says that all have sinned...including you. But the Bible also says that Christ died for sinners. Jesus took Barabbas' place in death...and He took yours as well. He paid for Barabbas' sins...and yours too. Hopefully you have responded to God's free gift of eternal life, bought and paid for by the blood of Jesus Christ. If not, open your heart to Him now. Accept His total forgiveness. Receive Him as your Savior.

Barnabas

The book of Acts mentions a man in the early church named Joseph, who was called Barnabas by the apostles. The Aramaic *bar naba* means "son of a prophet or prophecy or consolation." Luke, the writer of the book of Acts, translates Barnabas' name as "Son of Encouragement," a name Barnabas lived up to. It was Barnabas who first stood up for the apostle Paul when the believers in Jerusalem were afraid of him. They knew Paul had persecuted Christians, and they weren't sure if he really was a believer in Jesus or was masquerading as one. They thought Paul was trying to lull them into letting their guard down so he, a reknown Christian-hater, could haul them off to jail.

Barnabas became a respected leader of the church and later joined Paul on some of his missionary journeys. Before one trip, he and Paul separated when the two of them had a sharp disagreement over whether or not they should take John Mark, a young man who, for some unknown reason, abandoned them on an earlier trip. (See Acts 4:36; 15:36-41.)

A Life Lesson from Barnabas

Believing the Best About Others

We need more people like Barnabas today. Why? Because everyone needs encouragement…and an encourager. It's easy to criticize and slander others, but it's an act of love to positively build up others through encouragement. Barnabas believed in Paul when everyone else doubted him. Barnabas was correct, for Paul went on to write 13 books of the New Testament and plant many churches throughout the Roman world.

Barnabas also believed in John Mark's ability to faithfully serve Christ and the cause of the church when Paul didn't. The result? John Mark later joined Paul, and even Barnabas' missionary team, and even wrote one of the four Gospels.

Who can you single out to come alongside and encourage? Believing the best about another person is believing in God's power to change a life—any life. God hasn't given up on you, so don't you give up on others.

Did you know…?

Barnabas was one of the first people in the early church to sell his property and give the money to the apostles to be used for those in need.

Bible

The English word *Bible* comes from the Greek *ta biblia*, which means "the books." The Bible is literally a collection of books, all of which were breathed out by God and are helpful in equipping His people for every good work. All the books of the Bible have been "canonized" or officially recognized as divinely authoritative. (See 2 Timothy 3:16-17.)

How was the Bible written, and what is its message? The 66 books of the Bible were written over the course of 3500 years or so by an assortment of different authors living in different times in the ancient Middle East. Miraculously, all these books present a unified message: God created us and loves us in spite of our rebellion against Him, and He wants us to come into right relationship with Him. God proved His amazing love for us by the fact that Jesus died for us while we were still sinners. (See Romans 5:8.)

Is the Bible intended for us today? Absolutely! Although the individual books of the Bible were written with specific audiences in mind, the Bible is for us today as well. God orchestrated the production of the Scriptures, and He used each of the authors to bring forth the message He wanted to communicate to the whole world.

What does 2 Timothy 3:16-17 mean when it says that the Bible is breathed out by God, or God-breathed, or inspired by God? Simply stated, the Greek words that give us the meaning of these English words mean God's spirit or wind or breath. In other words, the Bible is inspired or breathed out by God. It came to us as the Holy Spirit guided the biblical writers through their individual personalities to compose what they wrote.

A Life Lesson About the Bible

God Is Not Silent

If you wanted others to know something about you, how would you let them know? You could leave visible clues of your existence, such as paintings or structures you had built, or you could write a letter or send an email. Well, God did some of these same things to let you know about Him. All creation—God's handiwork—speaks of His existence. But a more tangible piece of proof is the Bible, written by God Himself, the only book that claims to be—and is—inspired by God. The Bible records the beginning and the end of all time and all things. It accurately registers God's story of hope and salvation. Any honest seeker will have his doubts answered if he will simply read God's message. If you're doubting God's existence, read the Bible and learn about Him. If you are a believer in Him, read the Bible to discover and understand God's instructions to you. The Bible is His roadmap for your life.

The Bible is alive, it speaks to me.
—MARTIN LUTHER

Blood of Christ

In Old Testament times, the blood of bulls and goats was used to atone for the sins of the Israelites. The deaths of these animals served as replacements for the people's lives to symbolically absolve them of their sin. But this all changed with the coming of Jesus Christ. In the New Testament, Jesus offered up Himself in death. On the eve of His death (during which His blood would be shed), He instructed His disciples at what is generally referred to as "the Last Supper" that His blood would usher in a new covenant, that His blood would be shed for many for the remission of sins. Jesus knew He was going to die soon, and His blood would provide the atonement that the Old Testament animal sacrifices couldn't provide. The Bible is clear when it states that it is not possible for the blood of bulls and goats to take away sins. The blood of the perfect Son of God, Jesus Christ, however, is the perfect substitution for the death we deserve because of our sin. (See Leviticus 17:11; Matthew 26:27-28; Hebrews 10:4.)

Burning Bush

When Moses was tending his father-in-law's sheep in Midian, he led them out to the desert to Mount Horeb (also known as Mount Sinai). There he encountered a bush that burned, yet was not consumed by the fire. As Moses turned to see what was going on, God called to him from inside the bush. He told Moses to take off his sandals because he was standing on holy ground. God then explained to Moses that He had heard the cries of the people of Israel, who were in bondage in Egypt, and that He was going to use Moses to confront Pharaoh and bring His people out of Egypt.

Moses thought there was no way God could use him. He basically asked God, "Who am I? Why would You send me to go before Pharaoh? And what makes You think I could bring the children of Israel out of Egypt? No, God. You've got the wrong guy!" (See Exodus 3:11). God assured Moses that He would be with him. But Moses remained unconvinced that he was the right man for the job, even after God provided him with miracles to show the people confirmation that God had sent him. Moses wanted God to send someone else, but God refused, allowing only Aaron, Moses' brother, to go with him. Eventually, Moses complied and prepared to leave Midian to go to Egypt. (See Exodus 3:1-21.)

A Life Lesson in Following God

Stop, Look, and Listen

The mind plays funny tricks on a person in a desert environment. Moses saw something that looked like a burning bush, yet it was not consumed by the flame. Moses had spent 40 years in the desert and had never seen anything like this! He could have concluded that it was a mirage or that he was having a heat stroke, and returned to his tent. But the supernatural caught his attention and he went to investigate. This choice to turn and check out this strange happening turned Moses' life upside down. He was never the same person again.

Is God wanting to speak to you from His Word or through wise counsel? And are you willing to take the time to turn aside and hear His message? What if Moses hadn't paused and turned to receive God's instruction? Perhaps God would have found someone else, and Moses would have lost the blessing. Follow Moses' example: Stop, look, and listen to what God has to say to you. You'll be glad you did!

C

Caiaphas

Caiaphas was the Jewish high priest the year Jesus was crucified. He was educated, experienced, and skilled at problem-solving and persuasion. He was also an accomplice in the plot to have Jesus killed, using his position and all of his skills and abilities to convince others to arrest and execute the Son of God. After Jesus miraculously raised Lazarus from the dead, the chief priests and Pharisees convened a council to discuss the matter of what to do with Jesus. The Pharisees were afraid that Jesus' popularity would invoke Rome's wrath against them. Caiaphas scolded the Pharisees for their fear, explaining that it was better for them for one man to die for the people instead of the whole nation perishing. Caiaphas is a case of God using an evil man for His purpose. In this instance, God used the high priest's words as a prophecy regarding the substitutionary nature of Jesus' death. (For Caiaphas' story, see Matthew 26:57-68 and John 18:12-28. See also John 11:49-50.)

Cain

Cain was the firstborn son of Adam and Eve and the older brother of Abel. Because Abel gave God an acceptable sacrifice and Cain didn't, Cain became jealous of Abel and killed him in cold blood. God confronted Cain for his crime, cursing him to wander the earth as a fugitive. Cain complained to God that if anyone happened to find him, they would kill him. God replied that whoever would kill Cain would suffer terrible consequences. God then put a mark on Cain to keep people from killing him. Cain left God's presence and settled in the land of Nod, to the east of Eden, which is apparently where he met his wife. Cain had a son named Enoch, after whom he named a city he built. (For Cain's story, see Genesis 4:1-17.)

Did you know...?

The mark God put on Cain was a sign to warn cruel and violent troublemakers not to kill Cain. Whoever killed Cain would be severely punished by God Himself. God's mark also serves as a reminder that He cares for even the worst of criminals, even those like Cain, who murdered his own brother. God is in the business of extending His love and mercy to the undeserving. God doesn't give up on people, and neither should you.

Bare Bones Background

A few facts about Cain:

- ▶ The first human ever born
- ▶ The first murderer
- ▶ A farmer by occupation
- ▶ Name means "to acquire" or "to get"

Canaan

Canaan was the grandson of Noah, and the land that came to bear his name is now modern-day Israel and Palestine. Canaan as a land was first mentioned in Genesis 11:30-32 when God told Abraham to leave his own people and settle in a new land, called Canaan. Canaan would become the land God promised not only to Abraham but also to Isaac, Jacob, and their descendants forever. Moses would later lead the people of Israel from Egypt to this place also known as the Promised Land.

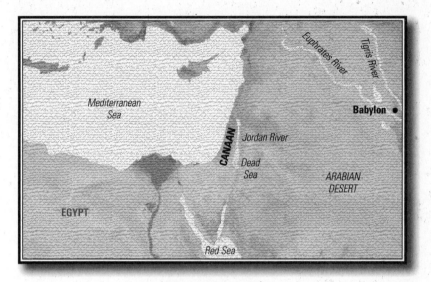

The Land of Canaan

Cherubim

A cherub is usually depicted in paintings and sculptures as a beautiful, innocent-looking, chubby, rosy-cheeked, winged child. Cherubim (the plural of *cherub*) are first mentioned in the Bible in the story of Adam and Eve, where they are referred to as the guardians of the way to the tree of life. They are described as appearing like human beings, having wings, and, in some special way, attending to God, who has

His throne above them. Golden cherubim were molded and placed on either end of the mercy seat above the Ark of the Covenant. Images of cherubim were also embroidered on the veil in the temple and were used in the adornment of various other parts of the temple. Also, the four living creatures mentioned in connection with Ezekiel's chariot are usually interpreted as cherubim.[4]

Did You Know...?

There is another order of angelic creatures called *seraphim*, meaning "to burn." These creatures bear a physical similarity to cherubim. They are agents of cleansing, as evident by the seraphim who put a burning coal on Isaiah's tongue. They have six wings—two to cover their face, two to cover their feet, and two for flying. (See Isaiah 6:2,6-7.)

Christ

The Greek *christos* (Christ) is a translation of the Hebrew *mashiach* (Messiah). So when Scripture calls the Son of God "Jesus Christ" or "Christ Jesus," it is making a theological claim about Him. As the Messiah, Jesus' mission was not merely political (as was the common expectation of the age), but greater than that. His mission was to save the people of Israel and the rest of the world from their sins. When Jesus went to the synagogue in Nazareth and read from Isaiah 61 about the anointed one God would send to minister salvation and comfort, He announced that He was that one, the fulfillment of Isaiah's prophecy. Jesus was the messianic deliverer promised in the Hebrew Scriptures. After the disciple Andrew discovered who Jesus was, he went to his brother Simon and told him he had found the Messiah, which translated means "Christ." The Old Testament is filled with prophecies of the coming of Jesus, the Christ, the Messiah. (See *Anointed One* and Isaiah 53; John 1:41; Isaiah 61:1-2; Luke 4:16-21.)

The Coming of Jesus the Messiah

Old Testament Predictions	*New Testament Fulfillments*
Micah 5:2—His birthplace in Bethlehem	Matthew 2:1-6
Isaiah 7:14—His virgin birth	Luke 1:34-35
Isaiah 7:14—His coming as Immanuel, "God with us"	Matthew 1:20-23
Zechariah 9:9—His triumphal entry into Jerusalem	Matthew 21:1-11
Isaiah 50:6—The physical abuse of Him during His trial	Matthew 27:30; John 19:3
Genesis 3:15—His triumph over Satan	Luke 4:14-15

> "There is born to you this day in the city of David
> a Savior, who is Christ the Lord"
> (LUKE 2:11).

Church

When we think of church, we often think of a building of some kind. But the Greek term *ekklesia* (which we translate as "church") does not refer to an edifice. It means "assembly"—specifically, an assembly of believers in Jesus. This can refer to a specific localized body of believers, or it can refer to all believers collectively (as is the case in 1 Corinthians 15:9).

Four Purposes of the Local Church

1. Exaltation of Jesus Christ
2. Evangelism of the lost
3. Edification of believers
4. Expression of service[5]

Circumcision

Circumcision was widely practiced by many nations throughout the Middle East. In Judaism, however, circumcision served as a sign of God's covenant with Abraham. It was a sign that from Abraham would come many nations and that God would give Abraham and his descendants the land of Canaan forever (Genesis 17). In the New Testament, circumcision often came into conflict with the concept of grace. Some Jewish believers told Gentiles they had to be circumcised and observe the Mosaic law if they wanted to become a Christian. However, the apostle Paul said that for Gentiles (or anyone) to accept circumcision as part of their salvation or standing before God was to disregard the grace provided by Christ through His death on the cross (Galatians 5:2-4). This biblical view held by Paul was affirmed by the Jewish leadership at a special meeting held in Jerusalem in Acts 15. (See Genesis 17; Galatians 5:2-4; Acts 15.)

Clothing of the Bible

In Bible times, most people made their own clothes. Clothing, garments, and fabrics were also prizes and plunder taken in battle. For the Israelites, there were some restrictions on what they were permitted to wear. God forbade the people of Israel from mixing fibers in their garments, and He condemned the practice of men wearing women's clothing and women wearing men's clothing.

Below are some examples of clothing worn in Bible times, some of which are still worn today. (See Leviticus 19:19 and Deuteronomy 22:5.)

Skin garments. After Adam and Eve sinned, they were ashamed at their nakedness and sewed fig leaves together for coverings. God then improved on their clothing by making garments of skin for them. Skin garments were probably common during the earliest days of history, especially among the poor. Two examples of those who wore garments from animal skins were the prophets Elijah and John the Baptist. (See Genesis 3:7,21; 2 Kings 1:8; Matthew 3:4.)

Robes. Also known as a mantle, the robe was the Israelite outer article of clothing, usually made of wool. Joseph's many-colored coat was probably a mantle. Jesus' own robe was a tunic without seams, probably woven whole on a particular type of loom with a hole for the head and two openings for the arms. According to the historian Josephus, the high priest also probably wore a seamless robe woven in this manner. A woman's robe was typically more intricate and of finer quality than a man's. (See Genesis 37:3; Job 1:20; John 19:23.)

Flavius Josephus (also known as Yosef Ben Matityahu) was a first-century Jewish historian who eventually became a Roman citizen. Josephus wrote extensive eyewitness accounts of Judaism and history during the first century A.D., which have provided many insights into life in Israel during that era.

Shoes and sandals. Sandals (Greek=*sandalion*) consisted of soles typically made of leather or wood and were tied onto the feet with thongs.

Men and women generally wore the same kinds of sandals, but those worn by women were more ornamental. Because sandals were not worn at home, putting them on indicated that it was time to walk somewhere. A pair of sandals could easily be worn out by a long journey.

Belts. A man's belt was made of leather, and a woman's belt was made of silk or perhaps wool and was more colorful.

Headdress. Sometimes men would wear turbans or caps to protect themselves from the sun. Women also wore headdresses, and theirs were generally far more colorful and made of lighter material.

Religious clothing. God mandated that His people bind His commandments around their hands and foreheads (Exodus 13:16; Deuteronomy 6:8; 11:18). Jewish tradition took this literally. *Phylacteries* (from the Hebrew word *t'filah,* indicating prayer) were a pair of black boxes which, according to Jewish tradition, needed to contain God's commandments.[6] God commanded Moses to tell the people of Israel to put a tassel or fringe on each corner of their garments, and each tassel was to have a blue thread. These tassels were to serve as reminders for the people to follow God's commandments and not follow after their own hearts or minds. The high priest of Israel wore an ephod—a priestly vestment decorated with 12 gemstones—attached to the breastplate of his garment, symbolizing God's providence and the priest's position. (See Exodus 13:16; Deuteronomy 6:8; 11:18; Numbers 15:38-40.)

Colosse

Colosse was a city located about 100 miles east of Ephesus, situated on the Lycus River. It was in the middle of what is now modern-day Turkey. This town was influential and important in its day. It was a crossroads where not only goods were traded and sold, but ideas and religious beliefs were exchanged, discussed, and introduced. Many Jews had fled from Jerusalem to Colosse due to persecution by Antiochus III and Antiochus IV about 200 years before Christ.

A man named Epaphras was probably the founder of the church there. Due to outside influence, false beliefs began to creep into the church at Colosse. This caused the apostle Paul to write a letter to the church—the book of Colossians in the Bible. He wrote to point out false teaching to those in the church and remind them of the supremacy and sufficiency of Christ and Christ alone. (See Colossians 1:7.)

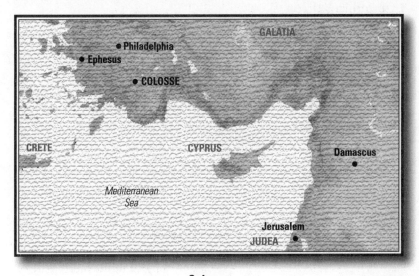

Colosse

Communion

During His last Passover meal on earth, Jesus broke bread (*matzah*, or unleavened bread), gave a blessing, and instructed His disciples to eat the bread, referring to it as His body. Next He told them to drink from a cup of wine, referring to it as the blood of the new covenant for the remission of sins. This last Passover meal became the basis for what Christians now celebrate as "communion." The apostle Paul explained this event to the Corinthians when he described how the bread and wine represented Jesus' broken body and spilled blood for the forgiveness of their sins. He then exhorted believers to share in the bread and drink from the cup. In so doing, they would be proclaiming the Lord's death until His second coming. That's why Christians take communion or the Lord's Supper today—to remember and give thanks for Jesus' death on our behalf. (See Matthew 26:26; 1 Corinthians 11:26.)

Names Used for Communion

Name	Meaning
The Lord's Supper	Indicates "remembrance" of the Passover meal Jesus shared with His disciples
Eucharist	Signifies "thanksgiving" because in communion we give thanks for Jesus' death on our behalf
Communion	Points to the "sharing" we enjoy with God and others who trust and believe in Him

Corinth

Corinth, a large city of Greece located southwest of Athens, was a bustling metropolis of the ancient Greco-Roman world. It was known for its rampant immorality and decadence. Corinth was also famous for its temple to Aphrodite, the Greek goddess of beauty. Corinth also had more than a dozen other pagan temples, fully staffed with hundreds of prostitutes.

The apostle Paul stayed in Corinth for 18 months during his second missionary journey. It was in Corinth he met Priscilla and Aquila, a couple who took him into their home and became powerful partners in sharing the gospel of Christ. In time, Paul wrote two letters to the believers in Corinth—1 Corinthians and 2 Corinthians—to correct their problems, mend their division, answer their questions, and instruct them on how to stay moral in an immoral environment... which Corinth certainly was!

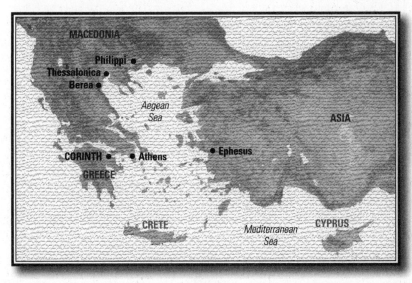

Corinth

What God Has Given You
for Staying Moral in an Immoral World

According to 1 Corinthians 1:2-9...

- He has cleansed you from sin.

- He has separated you from the world.

- He has given you His grace.

- He has made you spiritually rich in every way.

- He has promised to keep you strong to the end.

Covenant

In the Bible, a covenant (Hebrew=*b'rit*) was a contractual agreement between two parties. It was a legally binding obligation or promise. The Hebrew term conceptually denotes a "cutting" action. When the Bible states that God made a covenant, it literally means "he cut a covenant" (*karat b'rit*). God's covenant with Abraham, for example, was sealed by the symbolic action of a flaming torch and smoking oven passing through the pieces of animals that God had asked Abraham to cut in two. Some covenants were unconditional, meaning God would keep His end of the promise no matter what, and others were conditional, meaning God promised to keep His end of the promise if the people kept theirs. (See Genesis 15.)

The major covenants instituted by God in Scripture are:

- ▶ Noahaic Covenant—God promised to never again destroy the world with water (Genesis 9:8-15)

- ▶ Abrahamic Covenant—God promised the land to Abraham's descendants (Genesis 12:1-3)

- ▶ Sinaic Covenant—God gave the Israelites the law and instituted a judicial system (Exodus 19–24)

- ▶ Davidic Covenant—God promised that a descendant of David would always rule on the throne of David (2 Samuel 7:12-16)

- ▶ New Covenant—God promised a new spiritual relationship with individuals (Jeremiah 31:34; Matthew 26:28)

Thank God for His new covenant. Today you no longer must approach God through a priest and an animal sacrifice. No, you can go boldly and confidently to God through faith in His Son Jesus Christ, who was the perfect, final, and ultimate sacrifice. Jesus' death on the cross makes you acceptable to God. Because of His sacrifice, your sins are forgiven...if you believe in Him.

Cross

The cross was a cruel instrument of capital punishment. Rome executed its worst criminals on a cross, and Roman citizens were exempt from execution on a cross. Because the cross was such a vile form of punishment, it was reserved for the worst of the worst. *Crucifixion* comes from two Latin words meaning "fixed to a cross."

After Jesus was arrested, the Jewish religious leaders accused Him of blasphemy, which was punishable by death by stoning. But the Jewish people were not permitted under Roman rule to carry out death sentences, even though stoning probably did occur. Therefore the Jewish leaders incited a crowd of people to demand that Jesus be executed by the Romans as an enemy of Rome. To pad their case, the Jewish leaders affirmed that Jesus claimed to be God, which was a violation of Roman law, which stated that Caesar was god. Pilate, the Roman governor in the region, was pressured to sentence Jesus to death. He is the one who handed Jesus over to Roman soldiers, who nailed His wrists to the crossbeams of the cross. They also nailed His feet to the vertical beam of the cross. The cross was then raised up and dropped into a hole, leaving Jesus exposed to the elements. Death by crucifixion was excruciatingly painful, and most victims generally died of suffocation as body fluids built up in the lungs. However, Jesus willingly handed over, or gave up, His spirit and died. No one took His life from Him; He voluntarily dismissed it and gave up His life. (See Matthew 26:65; Mark 15:6-15; Leviticus 24:16; John 18:31; 19:30.)

A Life Lesson from the Cross

Making the Cross Personal

Because of sin, all mankind has fallen short of the glory of God (Romans 3:23), which means that all people—including you—deserve God's wrath. But God sent His Son Jesus to die and pay the penalty for the sins of those who believe in Him (John 3:16; Romans 5:9). The cross was simply the instrument by which Christ's death was accomplished. The cross is now empty, signifying that the penalty has been paid. Have you accepted Christ's death on your behalf? The price has been paid. Why not accept God's offer of forgiveness through Jesus Christ?

D

Damascus

The city of Damascus, located in Syria, is one of the most ancient of biblical cities. It was a key commercial center about 150 miles northeast of Jerusalem. Eliezer, Abraham's servant, was from Damascus. The apostle Paul traveled to Damascus to arrest followers of Jesus, only to have his journey cut short and changed forever by an encounter with the risen Jesus Himself on the road to Damascus. (See Genesis 15:2; Acts 9:1-27.)

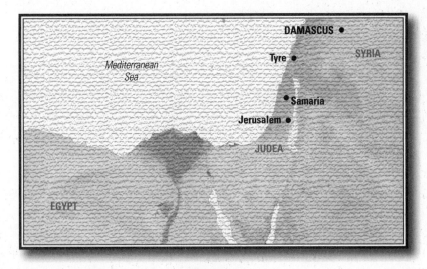

Damascus

Daniel

Daniel is an autobiographical book of the Bible, and he is a significant person in the Bible. Daniel (meaning "God is my judge") was just a teenager from the southern kingdom of Judah when he was taken to Babylon as a captive in 605 B.C. by King Nebuchadnezzar. Once there, he was given a new name and became known as Beltashazzar, meaning "he whom Bel favors." By giving Daniel this name, Nebuchadnezzar was trying to shift Daniel's loyalty from Jehovah, Judah's God, to Babylon's god. His plan failed miserably! (See Daniel 1:1-21.)

Daniel was a righteous man who avoided any and all compromise. Because of his moral soundness and God-given wisdom, he was placed in high positions in the Babylonian and Persian governments. Daniel also became a trusted interpreter of dreams. Not only did he make sense of King Nebuchadnezzar's dreams, but he also interpreted the mysterious handwriting on the wall that predicted King Belshazzar's fall. The book of Daniel is a record of the life and times of one of the most righteous men in the Old Testament. Because Daniel was of such stellar character, God called him "greatly beloved" three times, and revealed things to Daniel that would happen in the distant future and during the end times. (See Daniel 5:13-30; 9:23; 10:11,19.)

Daniel maintained a steadfast commitment to God for the rest of his life in a faraway, pagan land. He remains well known as a man who was faithful to God even when his life was threatened and he was thrown into a lions' den. God delivered His faithful servant Daniel from the lions' den, and Daniel's evil accusers and their families were killed in his place. (See Daniel 6:18-24.)

A Life Lesson from Daniel

Portrait of Commitment

Daniel shows that you can trust God even in times of great adversity. Throughout his long life, Daniel remained totally committed to God despite serving in political capacities within secular and heathen societies. He was a person of great integrity and faith whose total honesty and loyalty won him the respect and admiration of powerful pagan rulers. Daniel's prayerful relationship with God enabled him to live uncorrupted and exert great influence at the center of two world powers for over 80 years! Daniel trusted God and was totally committed to serving Him regardless of the cost. Because of his devotion to God, Daniel...

- refused to defile himself with the king's food
- prayed for God's insight into the king's dream
- gave praise to God in public
- confronted the king about his pride
- prayed despite the king's decree that no one should pray to God
- asked for God's forgiveness for himself and the people

Daniel provides an inspiring model of how to stand up for God in a secular society. Follow Daniel's example. Commit yourself to standing for truth and righteousness. Faithfully serve those in authority over you. Pray regularly. Be willing to suffer for God. Do this, and you will make a difference in your relationships, your community, and beyond.

David

When Saul, the first king of Israel, was disobedient to God, the prophet Samuel announced that the Lord had searched for a man after His own heart and had found him and appointed him as ruler over His people (1 Samuel 13:14). God eventually revealed this "man after His own heart" to be the youngest son of Jesse the Bethlehemite—David. David is known for being a shepherd boy, a singer and musician, a poet, a giant killer, a warrior, a king, and an adulterer.

It's obvious David was by no means perfect. Nevertheless, throughout the Hebrew Scriptures, God promised that a son from David's line would rule on David's throne forever. That promised son was the Messiah, Jesus of Nazareth. (David's life story spans 1 Samuel 16–1 Kings 2.)

Top 10+1 Facts About David

1. Was an ancestor of Jesus Christ
2. Considered to be the greatest king of Israel
3. Heralded as a man of faith (Hebrews 11)
4. Said by God to be a man after God's own heart
5. Committed adultery with Bathsheba
6. Slew the giant Goliath as a teenager
7. Arranged the murder of one of his soldiers
8. Remained a best friend to Jonathan, King Saul's son
9. Married Michal, King Saul's daughter
10. Took a census of the people, causing 70,000 men to die
11. Suffered an attempt by his son Absalom to overthrow his throne

A Life Lesson from David

Matters of the Heart

As the youngest son in his family, David was assigned to watch over the sheep. During these early days and nights spent alone, David developed a reverence for God. This respect for God as Creator often found its way into his psalms. (For an example, see Psalm 19.) Yet in David's life we find contradiction. He loved God, but he also sinned grievously against God's law. How do we understand such contradiction? First, the great David was just a man. He had the same sin nature every human possesses. Second, God understood the imperfect nature of David's love for Him. It's obvious God wasn't looking for perfection. He was looking for progression. God looked into David's heart and saw a man who, even though he failed at times, truly desired to obey and follow Him.

What does God see as He looks into your heart? It's no surprise He sees a sinner's heart right along with everyone else's. That's a given. But does He also see a seeker's heart? The heart of one who truly desires to obey—a progressing heart?

David by the Numbers

David had:

    7 brothers

    8 wives

He also:

    wrote 73 psalms

    was anointed 3 times

    served 40 years as king

    lived 70 years

Devil

The descriptions (see *Satan*) given to him in the Bible:

- The anointed cherub (Ezekiel 28:14)
- The ruler of demons (Luke 11:15)
- The god of this world (2 Corinthians 4:4)
- The prince of the power of the air (Ephesians 2:2)

Twelve

The ruler of this world (John 14:30)

- Beelzebub, the ruler of the demons (Matthew 12:24)

- A roaring lion (1 Peter 5:8)

The activities ascribed to him:

- Opposing God's work (Zechariah 3:1)

- Perverting God's Word (Matthew 4:6)

- Hindering God's workers (1 Thessalonians 2:18)

- Obstructing God's message (2 Corinthians 4:4)

- Entrapping God's people (1 Timothy 3:7)

- Overpowering God's children (1 Peter 5:8)

- Holding the world in his power (1 John 5:19)

- Heading ultimately into the lake of fire (Revelation 20:10)

Disciples, Twelve

Very early in His ministry, Jesus had many disciples or followers who later left Him. But there were 12 men He chose as His primary group of students—Simon (Peter) and his brother Andrew, James the son of Zebedee and his brother John, Philip and Batholomew, Thomas and Matthew (the tax collector), James the son of Alphaeus and Thaddaeus, and Simon the Zealot and Judas Iscariot, the one who later betrayed Jesus. (See John 6:2; Matthew 10:1-4; Mark 3:16-19; Luke 6:13-16.)

A closer look at the 12 disciples reveals:

- *Peter* was known for being passionate and one who often acted or spoke before he thought (see *Peter*).

- *Andrew,* Peter's brother, introduced Peter to Jesus.

- *James* and *John* were brothers nicknamed the Sons of Thunder by Jesus. They were able to witness Jesus' transfiguration along with Peter.

- *Philip* introduced *Nathanael* (also identified as *Bartholomew*) to Jesus.

- *Thomas* is mostly known for his doubt ("doubting Thomas") of the resurrection until he saw the risen Jesus.

- *Matthew* (or *Levi*) was a tax collector who left his tax-collecting booth to follow Jesus when Jesus called him.

- *James,* the son of Alphaeus, is sometimes identified as James the Less.

- *Thaddaeus* is probably the same as *Judas* (not Iscariot) in John 14:22.

- *Judas* Iscariot was the one who betrayed Jesus with a kiss and later hanged himself out of guilt.

This initial handful of men heard Jesus' call, answered it, left all, and followed Him. Jesus required them to have a different mind-set and attitude.

What Does It Mean to Be a Disciple of Christ?

Then Jesus said to His disciples, "If anyone desires to come after Me, let him deny himself, and take up his cross, and follow Me. For whoever desires to save his life will lose it, but whoever loses his life for My sake will find it. For what profit is it to a man if he gains the whole world, and loses his own soul? Or what will a man give in exchange for his soul?" (Matthew 16:24-26).

Dwellings of the Bible

Throughout the Bible we read of different kinds of dwellings that people lived in. Some found shelter and safety in caves. Tents were a prominent and portable home to many, including pilgrims and nomads. (The patriarchs and the wandering children of Israel were tent-dwellers.) Houses in the ancient Near East were another form of dwelling and were often make of bricks or stones, sycamore beams, and were whitewashed. Larger houses were built in a quadrangle with a courtyard and often had a flat roof with a low protective wall. Such rooftops were used for social purposes, especially during cool summer evenings.

Wherever God's people live today, the hope and desire of their heart is to dwell in the house of the Lord forever. (See Psalm 23:6.)

E

Eden, Garden of

Today the word *oasis* could be used to describe the perfect, magnificent garden paradise referred to in the Bible as the Garden of Eden. Because the first rain did not occur until the flood in the days of Noah, this oasis was watered by a spring that was the source of four rivers (the Pishon, Gihon, Tigris, and Euphrates). The garden's location was given as eastward in Eden, possibly in the area of ancient Babylon. The Garden of Eden (*Eden* meaning "delight") was created by God and was the original home of Adam and Eve, our first parents. There they lived in the presence of God and experienced a perfect relationship with Him.

Eden was a paradise without old age, sickness, or death. The fruit of the trees which God planted in this garden was suitable for eating. Adam and Eve could have lived forever in this eternal bliss! Among the trees God planted in the Garden of Eden were the tree of life and the tree of the knowledge of good and evil. God's only restriction upon Adam and Eve was that they were not to eat from the tree of knowledge. Because Adam and Eve disobeyed God and ate the fruit of that tree, sin entered into the world, and they were expelled from the garden. As an act of mercy, God placed angelic beings called cherubim at the east of the Garden of Eden to keep Adam and Eve from eating from the tree of life and living in a cursed condition forever. Not until believers today reach heaven will they experience the sinless perfection that was first created in the Garden of Eden. (See Genesis 2:8-14; 3.)

Egypt

In the ancient world, Egypt was a force to be reckoned with. A powerful and advanced empire, to this day the pyramids stand as a testament to its former stature. The kings of Egypt were referred to by the title *Pharaoh*.

Egypt was where Abraham and his wife Sarah went to live when a famine struck the land of Canaan. Also, when Joseph's brothers sold him to traders, the traders took Joseph to Egypt, where a series of events led him to become the second-in-command of all Egypt. After Joseph's death, the descendants of Israel stayed in Egypt until a new Pharaoh arose who did not know about Joseph. The new Pharaoh turned the Israelites into slaves. God later sent Moses to Egypt to free the Israelites (see *Exodus*) and lead them out of Egypt.

In the New Testament, we read that Mary and Joseph took the child Jesus to Egypt to avoid Herod's order to kill all boys under the age of two in Bethlehem and the surrounding area. After Herod's death, the young family returned to their homeland and settled in Nazareth. (See Genesis 12:10-20; 37:28-50; 26; Matthew 12:13-15.)

Elijah

Elijah (meaning "Yahweh is my God") the Tishbite, a prophet of God from the settlers of Gilead, was used mightily by God during the reigns of the kings Ahab and Ahaziah. He not only helped a widow with her provisions and her son (whom God raised from the dead through Elijah), but he also challenged the corrupt King Ahab and the priests of the false god Baal on Mount Carmel. After God was demonstrated to be the true God and Baal a false one, Elijah then ordered the deaths of—and killed—the priests of Baal. The evil queen Jezebel, the wife of King Ahab, was furious when she heard about this, and ordered the death of Elijah. Frightened, Elijah fled to Mount

Sinai. There, God revealed Himself to Elijah and commanded him to go back to Damascus. God also chose Elisha to serve as an assistant and successor for the worn-out and discouraged Elijah. After warning Ahab and Jezebel of their future violent deaths and warning Ahaziah of his own death, Elijah was miraculously "taken up" or "carried" by a whirlwind to heaven in a chariot of fire drawn by horses of fire. (For Elijah's story, see 1 Kings 17:1–2 Kings 2:11.)

A Life Lesson from Elijah

Yahweh Is My God

Elijah was a man dedicated to God in a hostile society. He was bold and brave, but he was also human and succumbed to fear and depression. The moment of his greatest victory—the confrontation against the 450 priests of Baal—was also the moment he was shaken by the threats of Jezebel. In a fit of depression, he tried to hide. However, God—Yahweh—found His servant and dealt with His prophet's depression in a gracious way. God never rebuked Elijah. Instead, He ministered to Elijah and nurtured him back to wholeness and usefulness.

Even during his faltering moments, Elijah never veered from his devotion to God. Do you have your "ups and downs" when it comes to following God's will for your life? Like Elijah, you are not alone. And like Elijah, God will never give up on you. Follow Elijah's example. Serve the Lord faithfully and courageously. Keep your eyes on Him, even in defeat. Trust Him to nurture you back to usefulness and supply all you need to carry out your ministry.

Did you know...?

Only two people went to heaven without dying:

Enoch was the first (Genesis 5:21-14).

Elijah was the second (2 Kings 2:11-12).

Elisha

As Elijah's successor, Elisha took up his teacher's mantle (robe), which fell as Elijah was being taken up to heaven in a chariot of fire. From that moment on, Elisha continued Elijah's ministry as a prophet. He returned to Jericho and purified the spring of water there by casting salt into it.

Perhaps Elisha is most known for what happened when he was traveling to Bethel—along the way, some young men mocked him (2 Kings 2:23). Elisha cursed them, and two bears came out of the woods and mauled 42 of the men. On other occasions, Elisha predicted rain when Jehoram's army was thirsty, helped a widow, restored a woman's son to life, multiplied 20 loaves of barley to feed 100 men, told Naaman the Syrian how to cure his leprosy, and performed many other famous miracles. (See 1 Kings 19:16–2 Kings 13:20.)

A Life Lesson from Elisha

You Are Unique!

Elisha's life teaches that all ministry is significant. From a human viewpoint, Elisha didn't seem to have as important or as prominent a ministry as his mentor Elijah had. But in the economy of God, Elisha's contribution was important in its revelation of God's love for His people. You too have been called and gifted by God for a purpose and a ministry. Therefore, be on guard not to measure yourself against other people's abilities or the scope of their service. The role you play in God's plan is the role He has designed for you. That makes you unique! Be faithful to fulfill your role as Elisha did his. Your life is significant. Live it faithfully and wisely.

Elizabeth

As one of the "daughters of Aaron," Elizabeth—whose name means

"God is my oath"—was the wife of a priest named Zacharias (see *Zacharias*). Both she and her husband were righteous before God. One day the angel Gabriel appeared to Zacharias as he was performing his duties in the temple, and told him that Elizabeth would bear a son whose name would be John (see *John the Baptist*). This son would turn people back to God. Zacharias wondered out loud how he and Elizabeth could have a child due to their extreme old age. Because he didn't believe the angel's words, he lost his ability to speak. This ability was not restored until John's birth.

When Elizabeth became pregnant, she dropped out of the public eye for five months. She was amazed at how the Lord had shown her favor by blessing her with a child and removing the stigma of barrenness from her reputation, a real issue in her day. Elizabeth saw her pregnancy as an act of grace from God, which was the meaning of the name John—"Yahweh is gracious." John grew up to be the forerunner of Christ, the man who prepared the way of the Lord. (See Luke 1:5,19-20,25; 3:1-6.)

Other Highlights from Elizabeth's Life

- ▶ Was the cousin of Mary, the mother of Jesus (Luke 1:36)
- ▶ Encouraged Mary when she was pregnant with Jesus (Luke 1:42-45)
- ▶ Spoke to the crowd for her husband when Zacharias was unable to speak (Luke 1:60)
- ▶ Stood up to the crowd who wanted to name John after Zacharias, his father (Luke 1:60)

A Life Lesson from Elizabeth

Waiting on God

Elizabeth speaks to us across the ages. One of her key life messages is how to wait on God...while living without. There was something

Elizabeth desperately wanted—a child. But time passed, and so did the age of childbearing—and there was no child. Yet God's Word records forever that Elizabeth was righteous and godly, that she obeyed God's law and was blameless. These are superlative marks for someone who was denied her heart's desire. It's obvious Elizabeth used her waiting and wanting time growing closer to God, loving Him, being faithful to Him, walking with Him, serving Him, and pressing herself to Him. By the time Elizabeth's dream became reality and she held her precious baby, it's possible that she had learned to live without. What she had discovered while waiting was priceless, as was her deeper relationship with God.

What is it you want and don't have? What have you dreamed of and been denied? And how are you handling waiting on the Lord? God's will is good and acceptable and perfect. And His timing is perfect too. Wait on the Lord. Wait patiently for Him. Fix your gaze on Him...not on your hopes and dreams. And don't forget—God's grace is always sufficient. He gives you everything you need for whatever circumstance you face.

Emmanuel

See *Immanuel*.

Ephesus

Ephesus was the capital of the Roman province of Asia (in modern Turkey). The city was best known for its magnificent temple of Artemis, or Diana. The temple was considered one of the seven wonders of the ancient world. Ephesus was a centerpiece in the apostle Paul's strategy of planting churches in major areas. Not only was it a religious center and a center for the occult, but it was also an important political, educational, and commercial center, ranking with Alexandria in Egypt. On his third missionary journey, Paul spent three years in this important city planting a church and training up its leaders. The spread of the gospel message had such a great impact on business that the makers of silver shrines to the goddess Diana stirred up a riot that forced Paul to leave town (Acts 19:1–20:1). There is no record that Paul ever returned to Ephesus. He did meet with the elders of the church at Miletus while on his way to Jerusalem, and he wrote a letter to the Christians in Ephesus while in prison (see *Epistles: Ephesians*). (See Acts 19:1–20:1; Acts 20:17-38.)

Ephesus

Did you know...?

The Christians in the church at Ephesus were commended by Jesus in the book of Revelation for:

- working hard
- being patient

- standing against sin
- discerning false teaching
- enduring in spite of suffering

The believers in the church at Ephesus were rebuked by Jesus for:

- losing their first love for Christ
- doing good works for the wrong reasons
- failing to repent of their sins

(See Revelation 2:2-5.)

Epistles

In the New Testament portion of the Bible, after the four Gospels and the book of Acts, we find what are known as *epistles*—or letters—written to various churches or individuals. Most of the epistles were composed by the apostle Paul. James, Peter, John, and Jude also wrote some of these letters. Revelation, the last book of the New Testament, is not an epistle. It does, however, contain seven letters that were written to seven churches throughout the Greco-Roman world. Here is a list of all the epistles and some important information about each of them.

Romans

Theme: *The righteousness of God*

Paul's letter to the Romans was essentially a presentation about how we are saved by faith in Jesus. It also served Paul's purpose of introducing himself to a church he had not yet visited. One of the most succinct explanations of how one is saved is found in Romans 10:9-10, which says that "if you confess with your mouth the Lord Jesus and believe in your heart that God has raised Him from the dead, you will be saved. For with the heart one believes unto righteousness, and with the mouth confession is made unto salvation."

First Corinthians

Theme: *Christian conduct*

Paul wrote this strong, direct letter to a church at Corinth that was struggling with division, judgmental attitudes, immorality, and denials of the resurrection of the dead. Some of the most famous and familiar verses from the Bible are in chapter 13 of this letter. They make up what is often referred to as "the love passage," which is commonly read in wedding ceremonies. First Corinthians was not Paul's first letter to the Corinthians. In 1 Corinthians 5:9, he described a letter he had previously written, which has since been lost to us.

True Love
1 Corinthians 13:4-7

Love suffers long and is kind;
love does not envy;
love does not parade itself, is not puffed up;
does not behave rudely, does not seek its own,
is not provoked, thinks no evil;
does not rejoice in iniquity;
but rejoices in the truth;
bears all things, believes all things,
hopes all things, endures all things.

Second Corinthians

Theme: *Paul's defense of his apostleship*

In this letter, Paul addressed several topics. He explained his suffering, defended his ministry, and urged the Corinthians to forgive a man who had been caught in sin. Paul's tone in this letter was noticeably softer than in his previous one (1 Corinthians), commending the Corinthians for their repentance. He also wrote of Christ's sacrificial love for us, writing probably one of the most memorable verses of this epistle: "He made Him who knew no sin to be sin for us, that we might become the righteousness of God in Him" (2 Corinthians 5:21).

Galatians
Theme: *Freedom in Christ*

There was trouble brewing in the region of Galatia. This letter was not addressed to specific individuals or to a specific church. It was addressed in general to the churches of Galatia and was circulated from church to church. Some Jewish Christians were convincing Gentiles that in order to be Christians, they had to submit themselves to the Mosaic law—that is, they had to be circumcised and keep the Sabbath. Paul, a Jewish Christian himself, wrote this letter, perhaps his most passionate, to put a stop to this requirement for works. He argued that to accept such teaching would be to forsake the grace of God: "I do not set aside the grace of God; for if righteousness comes through the law, then Christ died in vain...In Christ Jesus neither circumcision nor uncircumcision avails anything, but faith working through love" (Galatians 2:21; 5:6).

Ephesians
Theme: *Blessings in Christ*

The first three chapters of Ephesians explain what God has done for us as believers in Christ. The last three chapters look at what God's grace compels us to do in response. Ephesians 2:8-10 nicely summarizes the main theme of the entire letter: "By grace you have been saved through faith, and that not of yourselves; it is the gift of God, not of works, lest anyone should boast. For we are His workmanship, created in Christ Jesus for good works, which God prepared beforehand that we should walk in them."

Philippians
Theme: *The joy-filled life*

Paul wrote this letter to the Philippians from prison. This is a very joyful letter from Paul, who believed the persecution he had endured actually furthered the cause of the gospel. Paul also learned to be content in any circumstance, saying, "I know how to be abased, and I know how to abound. Everywhere and in all things I have learned both to be full and to be hungry, both to abound and to suffer need. I can do all things through Christ who strengthens me" (Philippians 4:12-13).

Colossians

Theme: *The sufficiency of Christ*

In Colossians, Paul contrasted being in Christ with legalism and carnal living. Paul reminded the Colossians of what Christ had done for them: "It pleased the Father that in Him [Christ] all the fullness should dwell, and by Him to reconcile all things to Himself, by Him, whether things on earth or things in heaven, having made peace through the blood of His cross" (Colossians 1:19-20).

First Thessalonians

Theme: *Concern for the church*

Paul wrote this cheerful letter with great thanksgiving that the Thessalonians had received the gospel that had been preached to them. He also encouraged the Thessalonians by mentioning the good news Timothy had brought to him about their faith and love: "Comfort each other and edify one another, just as you...are doing" (1 Thessalonians 5:11).

Second Thessalonians

Theme: *Living in hope*

In this second letter to the Thessalonians, Paul discussed the last days, the man of lawlessness, and the need for Christians to stand fast. He encouraged the Thessalonians that the best way to make it through these trying times was to pray for the spread of the gospel and to keep a good work ethic: "Do not grow weary in doing good" (2 Thessalonians 3:13).

First Timothy

Theme: *Instructions for a young disciple*

Paul wrote this letter to Timothy, his son in the faith, whom he had left in Ephesus. In this epistle, Paul gave Timothy instructions about the structure of the church committed to Timothy's trust, some specific details about church leaders, and counsel regarding the conduct of men and women in the church. Paul also gave Timothy personal encouragement: "Let no one despise your youth, but be an example to the believers in word, in conduct, in love, in spirit, in faith, in purity" (1 Timothy 4:12).

Second Timothy

Theme: *A charge to faithful ministry*

When Paul wrote this second letter to Timothy, who was still in Ephesus, the time of Paul's death was drawing near. In this letter, Paul praised Timothy for his faith and gave him some final instructions. He wanted Timothy to remain loyal and gave him this exhortation: "Preach the word! Be ready in season and out of season. Convince, rebuke, exhort, with all longsuffering and teaching" (2 Timothy 4:2).

Titus

Theme: *A manual of conduct*

This letter was written by Paul to Titus, another son in the faith. Paul had left Titus in Crete to organize church leadership there. He gave Titus instructions similar to those given to Timothy (see *First Timothy* and *Second Timothy*), reminding Titus of the power of God's grace to teach us to "live soberly, righteously, and godly in the present age" (Titus 2:12).

Philemon

Theme: *Forgiveness*

Paul wrote this brief but powerful letter to a believer named Philemon. Its message concerned Philemon's runaway slave, Onesimus. Paul implored Philemon to forgive Onesimus and take him back as a brother, not a slave: "Perhaps he [Onesimus] departed for a while for this purpose, that you might receive him forever, no longer as a slave but more than a slave—a beloved brother, especially to me but how much more to you, both in the flesh and in the Lord" (Philemon 15-16).

Hebrews

Theme: *The superiority of Christ*

The anonymous writer of this letter wrote to Jewish believers who were suffering rejection and persecution from fellow Jews. The letter was written to encourage and give them confidence in Christ, their Messiah. The writer was concerned with Jewish believers specifically, but he also wrote to Gentile believers as well. He explained that Jesus is our eternal High Priest, who cleansed us of our sin. His death on the cross accomplished what the sacrificial system could not: The blood of bulls and goats could not pay for our sins, but Jesus' could—and did. His blood shed on the cross initiated the new covenant: "Without shedding of blood there is no remission" (Hebrews 9:22). Hebrews is also well known for what is sometimes referred to as "Faith's Hall of Fame" in chapter 11, which lists many famous figures in the Bible who are commended for their faith.

James

Theme: *Genuine faith*

James wrote to the "twelve tribes which are scattered abroad" (James 1:1)—that is, Jewish believers. This James was the half-brother of Jesus, who was originally skeptical of Jesus' claims. Later he changed his view when Jesus appeared to him after His resurrection.

James had great authority in the church in Jerusalem (see Acts 15). He opened his letter with encouragement for those who were facing many trials, telling them to count the trials as pure joy. He also warned about favoritism, temptation, merely hearing the word but not doing it, and the danger of the tongue. Perhaps he is best known for his exhortation to show your faith by your works: "What use is it, my brethren, if someone says he has faith but he has no works? Can that faith save him?" (James 2:14 NASB). (See James 1:1; Matthew 13:55-56.)

First Peter

Theme: *Responding to suffering*

Peter wrote this epistle to believers scattered abroad to encourage them as they suffered for the cause of Christ. He urged them not to suffer as evildoers: "Keep your behavior excellent among the Gentiles, so that in the thing in which they slander you as evildoers, they may because of your good deeds, as they observe them, glorify God in the day of visitation" (1 Peter 2:12 NASB).

Second Peter

Theme: *Warning against false teachers*

Second Peter is a more serious letter than 1 Peter. In this epistle Peter admonished believers to beware of false prophets and keep Scripture in mind as they prepared for the last days, when the heavens and the earth would be destroyed. Peter then pointed out that God had something wonderful in store after all that judgment: "We, according to His promise, look for new heavens and a new earth in which righteousness dwells" (2 Peter 3:13).

First John

Theme: *Fellowship with God*

John, the beloved disciple, wrote this letter to remind its recipients of the reality of Jesus and His forgiveness, truth, and love. His most dominant theme is love, emphasizing that we should love one another and love God because "He loved us and sent His Son to be the propitiation for our sins" (1 John 4:10).

Second John

Theme: *Christian discernment*

John wrote this letter to an anonymous "elect lady and her children," telling them to walk in the Messiah's commandments and beware of antichrist deceivers such as those who denied that Jesus had come to earth in a human body. Of them and those like them, John wrote: "Many deceivers have gone out into the world who do not confess Jesus Christ as coming in the flesh. This is a deceiver and an antichrist" (2 John 7). (See 2 John 1.)

Third John

Theme: *Christian hospitality*

John wrote this letter to "the beloved Gaius" and commended him for his faith and generosity. He also had some difficult things to say about a man named Diotrephes, who had a tendency to lord over others. John sternly warned his audience, "Beloved, do not imitate what is evil, but what is good. He who does good is of God, but he who does evil has not seen God" (3 John 11). (See 3 John 1.)

Jude

Theme: *Contending for the faith*

Jude was one of Jesus' half-brothers. His letter urged passionate contending for the faith, warning of apostasy. He also recognized the importance of having mercy on those who might question the faith: "Have mercy on some, who are doubting; save others, snatching them out of the fire" (Jude 22-23 NASB). (See Matthew 13:55.)

Did you know…?

The Bible Made Simple

The message of Jesus Christ was…

…predicted in the Old Testament

…lived out in flesh in the Gospels

…spread in the book of Acts

…taught and explained in the epistles

Esau/Edom

Esau was the older brother of Jacob and the son of Isaac and Rebekah. Esau was born red and hairy, so they called him *Esau*, which means "hairy." As he grew, Esau became a skilled hunter and outdoorsman (Genesis 25:27), a big contrast to the mild-mannered, tent-dwelling Jacob. Isaac's favorite son was Esau, while Rebekah favored Jacob. Because Esau gave up his birthright to Jacob for a portion of red (Hebrew=*edom)* stew, Esau became known as Edom. As predicted or prophesied to Rebekah, Esau (Edom), the older brother, ended up serving his younger brother, Jacob (Israel). Edom and Israel became rival nations. Israel has survived to this day, but Edom has disappeared in history. (For Esau's story, see Genesis 25–36.)

Esther/Hadassah

Hadassah (whose name means "myrtle") was a young Jewish girl brought up during the reign of the Persian king Xerxes (or Ahasuerus). Her story takes place around 483 to 473 B.C. She was raised by her cousin Mordecai in the citadel of Shushan (or Susa), which was the capital of the Persian Empire during the winter months. Her Persian name, *Esther,* means "star," which was appropriate because she was lovely and beautiful.

When King Xerxes became displeased with his wife, Queen Vashti, his advisors suggested that a search be made for the most beautiful young virgins in the land. The king could then select a new queen from this choice group. Esther was the one chosen by the king to become the new queen. (See Esther 2:2-7.)

Soon an evil man named Haman rose to power under Xerxes and ordered that all Jews be killed. Esther then used her position as the favored queen to plead for the lives of her people. Esther's actions successfully exposed Haman's wickedness to the king, and Haman was hanged on the very gallows he had prepared for Mordecai's death. As a result of Esther's stand, the Jews were given the opportunity to defend themselves against Haman's decree. The feast of Purim, which is still celebrated to this day, was instituted to commemorate this event. (For Esther's story, see Esther 1–10.)

Did you know...?

Esther's most famous words are, "If I perish, I perish!"

The name of God is never mentioned in the book of Esther, but His activity is evident throughout.

(See Esther 4:16; 7:9-10.)

A Life Lesson from Esther

God's Formula for Success

Esther's external beauty was the vehicle God used to bring her into a place of important influence. But there was much more to Esther than her outer beauty. She also possessed a God-given grace and dignity that procured the favor of all those within the palace. Even after she was in the powerful position of queen, Esther continued to appreciate and heed the advice of her older cousin, Mordecai.

Esther's role in delivering the Jews from Haman's evil plot to destroy them was due to God's formula for success—a combination of His divine providence, Esther's physical attributes and practical wisdom, and the assistance and wisdom of others. The church, the Body of Christ, is comprised of people God has blessed with different spiritual gifts and varying degrees of spiritual maturity. These spiritually endowed and mature people have been placed around you to help and assist you in doing God's work and living out His will for you. Don't fail to draw on the resources God has provided.

Euphrates River

The Euphrates (meaning "fruitful") was one of the four rivers described in Genesis 2 as flowing out of the garden in Eden (see *Eden*). God had promised Abraham he would be given a land that stretched from the Nile River all the way to the Euphrates. Today the Euphrates River is 1728 miles long and flows through modern-day Turkey, Syria, and Iraq. (See Genesis 15:18; Deuteronomy 11:24; Joshua 1:4.)

Exodus

The exodus was an event in Jewish history in which the people of Israel were delivered by God through Moses from slavery in Egypt. After ten plagues from God, Pharaoh, the ruler of Egypt, finally let the enslaved Israelites go, and Moses and the people of Israel left Egypt for Canaan, the Promised Land. But Pharaoh later changed his mind and chased after the Israelites as they were approaching the Red Sea. God then made the waters part and the Israelites walked through the waters that stood like two walls on their right and left (Exodus 14:22).

After the Israelites were safely across, God let the waters crash down upon the Egyptians.

Then the Israelites journeyed to Mount Sinai (Horeb), where God presented Moses with the Ten Commandments. The people then continued on their journey to Canaan, the land God had originally promised to Abraham, Isaac, and Jacob. Unfortunately the Israelites feared the giant people in Canaan, and refused to obey God's command to take the land. Consequently God made an entire generation wander in the wilderness for 40 years, until they had died off. Only Joshua and Caleb believed God and lived to dwell in the land of Canaan along with the new generation of Israelites. It was Joshua, Moses' successor, who led the people into Canaan, conquering the evil people of the land. (To learn more about the Exodus, read Exodus 13:17–14:31.)

The Israelites left Succoth, and after crossing the Red Sea, stopped at the oasis in Elim. At Mount Sinai God gave the Ten Commandments. After disobeying God's command to enter Canaan, the people were sent to wander in the wilderness for 40 years.

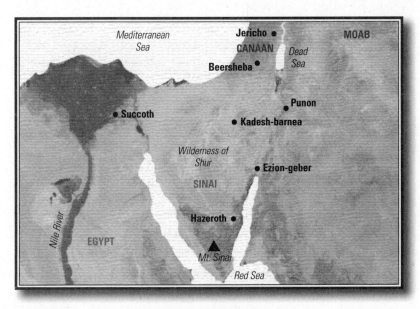

The Regions of the Exodus

Exiles

In ancient times, when a nation was defeated, many of its people were carried away in exile to the conquering land. These exiles were either used as slaves or provided skills that were in short supply in the victor's country. The divided kingdoms of Israel and Judah both experienced deportations as punishment from God for their disobedience.

▶ The northern kingdom of Israel was exiled to Assyria in 722 B.C. The northern kingdom of Israel ceased to exist. (See 2 Kings 15:29.)

▶ The southern kingdom of Judah experienced three deportations to Babylon: In 605 B.C. Daniel and many other youths of nobility were taken. (See Daniel 1:1-6.) In 597 B.C., Ezekiel and others were taken after the defeat of King Jehoiachin. (See 2 Kings 24.) In 586 B.C., Jerusalem was destroyed and most of the survivors were taken to Babylon. (See 2 Kings 25:8-11.)

Did you know...?

Jeremiah predicted that the exile of the southern kingdom of Judah would last for 70 years. That's precisely what happened! From 605 B.C. (the first deportation) until 536/35 B.C. (when Cyrus, the king of Persia and conqueror of Babylon, allowed some of the Jews to return to their homeland) was exactly 70 years. (See Jeremiah 25:11.)

F

Faith

Throughout the Bible, faith is defined as trust or belief. The patriarch Abraham had faith in God's promise to him that he would father many nations, and God credited this faith to him as righteousness. Genesis 15:6 became a foundational text for Paul, who contended that we are justified by faith and not by works of the law. Jesus often rebuked His own disciples for not having enough faith. James stressed that faith without works is dead. And Paul wrote that saving faith will result in good works—not to be saved, but as a product of genuine faith. Hebrews 11, often referred to as the Bible Hall of Faith, lists many biblical figures who were well known for their faith. (See Genesis 15:6; Romans 3:28; 4:3; Galatians 3:6; James 2:17.)

Saved to Serve

For by grace you have been saved through faith,
and that not of yourselves;
it is the gift of God, not of works,
lest anyone should boast.
For we are His workmanship,
created in Christ Jesus for good works,
which God prepared beforehand
that we should walk in them
(Ephesians 2:8-10).

Fall

Humanity's fall into sin is described in Genesis 3, when Eve was deceived by the serpent's cunning and took the fruit God forbade her to eat. She also gave some to Adam, and he ate as well, disobeying God. God confronted them both, and He expelled them from the Garden of Eden, where they had lived. It was because of the fall that sin spread to all mankind. Our sin separates us from God and condemns us to eternity apart from Him. God's answer to the fall was to send His Son, Jesus, to die on the cross and take the punishment of our sin upon Himself and rise again, thus conquering the power of sin. Those who believe in Christ as Savior will be saved and enjoy eternity in Christ's presence. (To learn more about the fall, read Genesis 3.)

Festivals of the Bible

The Jewish festivals or feasts are a rich part of Jewish culture. With the people scattered throughout the land, three annual feasts helped to unify the people both socially and religiously. These major festivals required all males to be present, and were joyful occasions commemorating the exodus from Egypt to the Promised Land. (See Exodus 23:14-17.)

The Feast of Unleavened Bread. This feast began the day after the Passover meal and required that the people eat only unleavened bread during the seven days of this feast. The purpose of this feast was to remember the time of the Passover and the exodus of God's people from Egypt. The Last Supper (which is recorded in the New Testament) was actually a Passover meal. It was there that Jesus symbolically took the unleavened bread and the wine and compared them to His body and blood. Theologically, Jesus was our Passover lamb—unblemished and perfect because of His sinless life, and sent to death on the cross to save us from God's wrath against our sin. (See Leviticus 23:4-8; Matthew 26:17-29.)

The Feast of Harvest. This feast was also called the Feast of Weeks. The Feast of Weeks occurred seven weeks, or "fifty days," after Passover. The first of the wheat harvest was offered at this feast. The Greek term *pentekostes* means "fifty," which is where we get the term Pentecost. In a Christian context, God poured out His Holy Spirit on Peter and the apostles on Pentecost. Peter preached a sermon to the pilgrims who had come to the Feast of Weeks or Pentecost, and they all heard Peter's sermon in their own language. On that day, 3000 people became saved! (See Leviticus 23:16; Numbers 28:26-31; Acts 2.)

Feast of Ingathering. This feast was also called Feast of Tabernacles or Booths. This feast started five days after Yom Kippur ("the Day of Atonement"), and lasted for seven days. An eighth day was added for physical rest. For the feast, Jewish families built temporary booths made of palm branches in order to commemorate God's provision for them in the wilderness when He took them out of Egypt. (See Leviticus 23:33-43.)

Other Feasts and Festivals

Type of Feast	Purpose of Feast
Firstfruits	to dedicate the initial part of the barley harvest to the Lord
Trumpets	to consecrate the seventh month as a sabbatical month
Day of Atonement	to annually point to the forgiveness and cleansing of sin for the priests, the nation, and the tabernacle

Dedication or Hanukkah	to celebrate the purification of the temple in 167 B.C.[7]
Purim	to annually commemorate the deliverance of the Jews from the massacre plotted by Haman in Esther 9

Flood

Because of the great wickedness of people in the days of Noah, God was sorry He had created them. Therefore He sent a flood that covered the entire earth so that every living thing on the earth would die. Only Noah and his family were spared because Noah found favor in the eyes of the Lord. To preserve Noah's family, God had Noah build a box-shaped ark that was equivalent in length to approximately one-and-a-half football fields, or about 150 yards. (See *Ark of Noah*.) Two of every kind of animal, male and female, were put into this boat, along with Noah and his family. The first-ever rain fell for 40 days and 40 nights. Noah and his family were in the ark for approximately 12 months and 11 days.

Ultimately the ark landed on a mountain in the region of Ararat. Noah tested whether there was any dry land by sending out a dove. The first sign of dry land was evidenced when the dove returned with an olive leaf in its beak. The final sign was when the dove did not return. Then God told Noah and his family to exit the ark and to be fruitful and multiply. God then promised to never again flood the earth. As a sign of that covenant, He made a rainbow. (To learn more about the flood, see Genesis 6:1–9:17.)

Foods of the Bible

In addition to the common elements of water and salt, both of which were vital in Bible times, here are some other foods found in the pages of Scripture:

Manna. When the Israelites complained about not having food while in the wilderness, God provided them with manna in the mornings. Manna is described as "a small round substance," or thin flakes "as fine as frost on the ground." When the Israelites first saw manna, they said to each other, *"Man hu?"* meaning "What is that?" This is how this food came to be called *manna.* It is also described as looking like small coriander seed, pale yellow in color. Whatever it was, it sustained the Israelites in the desert for 40 years. (See Exodus 16:14; Numbers 11:7.)

Wheat and barley. After the Israelites entered the land of Canaan and settled, they were able to plant crops. Wheat and barley were the dominant grains, which were used for cooking and baking bread. The people often plucked fresh grain from the field and shucked it before consuming it raw, and they also roasted grain. (See Matthew 12:1.)

Figs. The Middle East has always been well known for its abundant figs and their pronounced sweetness. Figs were eaten fresh and also dried in the sun and stored away for later use. High in calcium and fiber, they were often prepared in cake form to help sustain soldiers. (Some people have suggested that figs may have been the forbidden fruit in the Garden of Eden, since Adam and Eve used fig leaves to cover themselves, but no one knows for sure. Jesus also cursed a fig tree for failing to bear fruit [Matthew 21:19].) Figs are still a common food and delicacy in the Middle East today.

Kosher foods (or kashrut). The term *kosher* means "clean." In Jewish law, it applies to foods that are approved for Jews to consume. The dietary laws (*kashrut*) of the Old Testament found in Leviticus 11 prohibited consuming or touching the carcasses of certain animals such as camels, rodents, rabbits, or pigs. But any living thing in the water, as long as it had scales, was okay to eat. That is why, as Jews, Jesus and His disciples could eat fish, and His disciples could be fishermen by trade. But eagles, vultures, falcons, ravens, ostriches, and bats could not be eaten.

In the New Testament, God showed Peter through a dream that he should not call "unclean" that which God had made clean. These instructions included people who were non-Jews, who were considered to be unclean by many Jews during Peter's day. (Ultimately, the vision was not so much about food as it was about the inclusion of the Gentiles in the New Testament church.) To this day, many observant Jews will not touch or consume nonkosher foods. (See Acts 10:15. To learn more about kosher foods, see Leviticus 11.)

Other foods. In addition to the above-mentioned foods, olives, olive oil, honey, grapes, and pomegranates were available and consumed to sustain life.

Forgiveness

Forgiveness is a theme that runs through the entire Bible. In the Old Testament, Joseph forgave his brothers of the evil they did to him. God forgave David of his adultery with Bathsheba and his murder of her husband to cover his tracks. In the New Testament, Jesus offered forgiveness to all who place their trust in Him as Savior and Lord. He also urged His followers to forgive others. And the apostle Paul, in his writings, frequently wrote about the forgiveness of others. (See Exodus 50:19-21; Psalm 51:1,9; Matthew 18:21-22; Ephesians 4:32.)

A Life Lesson on Forgiveness

As God Has Forgiven You

"To err is human, but to forgive is divine" is a proverbial saying that implies it's easy to make mistakes yourself but hard to forgive the mistakes of others. Aren't you glad God doesn't possess this human tendency? Regardless of your past and your mistakes, God is ready to grant you forgiveness through His Son's death in payment for all your faults. Are you ready to accept His offer? And if you have received His forgiveness, show a spark of divinity and pass it on to others! As the Bible advises, forgive others just as God has forgiven you (Ephesians 4:32).

Dialogue Between Peter and Jesus

Peter: "Lord, how often shall my brother sin against me, and I forgive him? Up to seven times?"

Jesus: "I do not say to you, up to seven times, but up to seventy times seven."

(See Matthew 18:21-22.)

G

Galatia

Galatia was a region in the central section of what is modern-day Turkey. It was filled with Celtic people whose ancestors had migrated there. When the apostle Paul came to Galatia with Barnabas, many of the Galatians there began to offer sacrifices to them, mistaking them for the Greek gods Zeus and Hermes. Even when Paul and Barnabas tore their clothes and told the people of the real God they should be worshiping, they still had difficulty preventing the Galatians from offering sacrifices to them. (See Acts 14:11-18.)

Some people in Antioch, an important city in Galatia, were teaching that Gentiles had to become Jews and observe certain Jewish rituals before they could become Christians. This false teaching prompted Paul to write a letter to those in Galatia. In the Bible, this letter is the book of Galatians. (See *Epistles: Galatians.*)

Galatia

Galilee

This was the name given to the northernmost region of Israel. It is mentioned several times in the Old Testament. Jesus' hometown of Nazareth was located in Galilee. Capernaum, the town Jesus chose as the home base for His ministry, was also in Galilee. Because there were over 250 towns and many synagogues in Galilee, Jesus reached and taught large numbers of people in this region.

Garments

See *Clothing of the Bible.*

Gentiles

The term *Gentiles* originally meant "nations." In fact, the Hebrew word *goyim* and the Greek term *ethne* both mean "nations." Over time, *Gentiles* became understood to mean non-Jews or those belonging to nations other than Israel.

Did you know...?

- The Jewish nation—or people—believed they were "chosen" to be the only ones blessed by God. The Jews completely missed God's plan that they were to share God's blessings with the Gentiles—with all the nations (Genesis 12:3).

- Jesus ministered to non-Jews, which demonstrated that God's blessing was to include Gentiles. (For examples, see Matthew 8:5-13; Mark 7:24-30; John 4:27.)

- The blood of Christ has brought Gentiles near to God (Ephesians 2:11-13).
- All barriers dividing Jews and Gentiles were abolished in Christ (Ephesians 2:14).

Geography of the Bible

Rivers. The key rivers of the Bible include...

- the Tigris, along which Nineveh, the capital city of Assyria, was located.

- the Euphrates, which flowed through the Garden of Eden and where Babylon was situated.

- the Nile, where a basket containing the baby Moses was placed in order to save his life.

- the Jordan, the river God's people crossed to enter the Promised Land.

Mountains. Important mounts and mountains include...

- Mount Ararat, where Noah's ark rested.

- Mount Moriah, where Abraham offered up his son Isaac in obedience to God.

- Mount Sinai, where God gave Moses the Ten Commandments.

- Mount Carmel, where Elijah challenged the prophets of Baal.

- Mount Nebo, where Moses viewed the Promised Land, died, and was buried by God.

- Mount of Olives in Jerusalem, where God Himself will stand in the last days.

Valleys. Some of the named valleys include...

- the valley of Hinnom (just outside Jerusalem), where refuse was burned. This site provided the backdrop for much of Jesus' discussion of hell.

- the valley of Megiddo, where the earth's final battle, the battle of Armageddon, will be fought.

Seas and lakes. Some familiar seas and lakes include...

- the Mediterranean Sea, which borders the coast of Israel and other major locations described in the Bible, such as Egypt, Rome, and Greece.

- the Red Sea, sometimes called the Sea of Reeds, which God parted to free the Israelites from Egyptian bondage.

- the Dead Sea or the Salt Sea, near which the Dead Sea Scrolls were found. These scrolls contained accurate copies of certain Old Testament books of the Bible.

- the Sea of Galilee, a lake that is mentioned in connection with many events in the lives of Jesus and His disciples.

- lake of fire and brimstone, a prophetic place where Satan, the beast, the false prophet, and ultimately, death will one day be thrown forever.

Gideon

Gideon was a judge in Israel during a time when the nation was under the oppression of the Midianites because of Israel's disobedience against God. God used Gideon to destroy not only an altar of Baal (see *Baal*) but also to defeat the Midianites. Gideon asked God for a sign to let him know whether or not He would use Gideon to help save Israel. God showed Gideon that clearly this was so, and with 300 men—armed only with trumpets and torches hidden in clay pitchers—Gideon prevailed. Later, Gideon refused the people's offer to make him king, saying neither he nor his son would rule over the people, but the Lord God would rule over them. (See Judges 8:23. For Gideon's story, read Judges 6 and 7.)

A Life Lesson from Gideon

Are You Asking for a Sign?

Missouri is nicknamed "The Show Me State," and Gideon might as well have been from Missouri. Why? Because he wanted proof that he, Gideon, a simple farmer, could truly defeat the powerful Midianite army. Graciously, God gave him a sign, and more importantly, a dramatic victory.

Now, how about you? Most people think that if they were visited by God they would never be as weak as Gideon was, questioning and doubting God and asking for proof. But think about this: Every time you open God's Word and fail to respond in faith to His message, you are following in Gideon's faulty steps. If you want to have more of God's guidance, don't ask for signs. Ask for faith to believe and obey as you read God's revealed messages from His Word, the Bible.

God, Names of

Elohim: "God." First appearing in the opening verse of the Bible, *elohim* is plural, yet it is applied to a singular God. Whenever the word *elohim* is used of the one true God, it is accompanied by a singular verb. Its root (*el*) probably means "mighty one," which suggests God's great power. Scholars consider the plural ending (*-im*) to indicate a "plural of majesty"—that is, emphasizing the greatness of God. (See Genesis 1:1.)

- *Yahweh:* "He is." The English letters YHWH spell God's proper name, believed to be pronounced "Yahweh," which simply means "He is," implying God's self-existent nature. When God appeared to Moses through a burning bush and ordered him to bring the people of Israel out of Egypt, God told Moses to tell the people "I AM has sent me to you" (Exodus 3:14).

- *Adonai:* "Lord." This name for God first appears in Genesis 15:2 and means "God is the ruling Lord." The Hebrews would not pronounce the name of God—YHWH—out loud. Therefore every time this name of God appeared in the Hebrew text, they pronounced it *Jehovah*, a word made up of the vowels of Adonai and the consonants of YHWH.

- *El Elyon:* "God Most High." King Melchizedek of Salem was a priest of *El Elyon,* usually translated as "God Most High." Melchizedek proceeded to bless Abraham of God Most High, the possessor of heaven and earth. (See Genesis 14:18-20.)

- *El Roi:* "God who sees." After the angel of the Lord spoke to Hagar in the wilderness, He instructed her to return to Abraham and Sarah and said God promised to greatly bless her and that she would have a son named Ishmael. In response, Hagar called God *El Roi,* which means "God who sees" or "God of seeing"—an acknowledgment that God was watching and caring for her. (See Genesis 16:13.)

- *El Shaddai:* "God Almighty." This name is sometimes translated as "Almighty God." God first used this name for Himself when He spoke to Abram/Abraham, saying, "I am Almighty God," emphasizing His power to fulfill His promises. Most of the time *El Shaddai* is used, it is in connection with God's promise to Abraham that he would have many descendants. (See Genesis 17:1-6.)

- *Yahweh Yireh:* "The Lord will provide." This name appears in Genesis

22, where God commanded Abraham to sacrifice his son Isaac on Mount Moriah. When Abraham was about to kill his son, the angel of the Lord intervened and provided a ram to be used as a sacrifice in Isaac's place. Abraham called that place *Yahweh Yireh,* which means, "the Lord will provide." (See Genesis 22:14.)

Yahweh Tz'vaot: "Lord of hosts." This name of God emphasizes His amazing power. The Hebrew term literally means "armies," so Yahweh is pictured here as one who has access not to just one army, but legions of armies. In the New Testament, both Paul and James refer to this name of God. (See Isaiah 1:9; Romans 9:29; James 5:4.)

Something to Try...
Use the Names of God in Your Prayers

It's a great exercise to pray using the names of God. The next time you pray, instead of beginning your prayer with "Dear God" or "Dear Lord" or "Our Father," go a step further and begin your prayer by using one of these names of God.

Gospel

The "good news" (Greek=*euangelion,* from which we get the term *evangelism*) has been traditionally translated with the English word *gospel,* which comes from the Old English *gōdspel* ("good tale"). Thus the gospel is the good news.

What is the "good news"? First, the bad news: Mankind rebelled against God, which makes all people worthy of eternal death. But the good news is that Jesus, the long-awaited Jewish Messiah, came to earth to die on the cross in our place, rise again, and provide everlasting life

...elieve in Him—not just to Jews, but to anyone. Paul ...ospel is the power of God for salvation to everyone ...e Romans 1:16.)

The Gospel According to Romans
"The Roman Road"

The fact of sin—Romans 3:23: "All have sinned and fall short of the glory of God."

The fact of death—Romans 6:23: "The wages of sin is death, but the gift of God is eternal life in Christ Jesus our Lord."

The fact of God's love—Romans 5:8: "God demonstrates His own love toward us, in that while we were still sinners, Christ died for us."

The act of confession—Romans 10:9-10: "If you confess with your mouth the Lord Jesus and believe in your heart that God has raised Him from the dead, you will be saved. For with the heart one believes unto righteousness, and with the mouth confession is made unto salvation."

Gospels, Four

Introduction

The Gospels (Matthew, Mark, Luke, John) are the first four books in the New Testament. They are biographies of the life, death, and resurrection of Jesus the Messiah, written so that whoever reads them might believe in Him.

Matthew

Theme: *The Kingdom of God*

Matthew, whose Jewish name was Levi, was one of Jesus' 12 disciples. He was a tax collector who left all to follow Jesus when He called him. He wrote his Gospel to Jews, presenting Jesus of Nazareth as Israel's promised Messiah and rightful king—the King of kings. (See Matthew 9:9.)

Interesting Facts about the Gospel of Matthew

Only Matthew records:

- ▸ The visit of the wise men to worship Jesus.

- ▸ Joseph's dream that King Herod wanted to destroy the baby Jesus.

- ▸ The flight to Egypt by Joseph, Mary, and Jesus to save Jesus' life.

- ▸ The dream of Pilate's wife that he should have nothing to do with Jesus' trial.

- ▸ The bribery of the soldiers to lie about the angels who rolled away Jesus' gravestone.

- ▸ The Great Commission from Jesus to His disciples to go and make disciples of all nations.

Mark

Theme: *The Suffering Servant*

John, whose surname was Mark, was not an eyewitness of the life of Jesus. He was, however, a close companion of the apostle Peter, who passed on details and information about his association with Jesus to John Mark. Mark wrote his Gospel account from Rome and targeted Roman believers, appealing to their admiration of power and action.

Mark presented Jesus as the suffering servant. His focus was more on the deeds of Jesus than His teachings. He demonstrated the humanity of Christ and described His human emotions, His limitations as a human, and ultimately His physical death.

Interesting Facts About the Gospel of Mark

▶ It is the shortest of the four Gospels.

▶ It contains no genealogy of Jesus.

▶ It features the miracles of Jesus more than His teachings.

▶ It records more miracles than any other Gospel.

> "Even the Son of Man did not come to be served, but to serve, and to give His life a ransom for many"
> (MARK 10:45).

Luke

Theme: *The Perfect Man*

Luke, a doctor and the only Gentile (non-Jew) author among the New Testament writers, wrote to strengthen the faith of Gentiles, especially Greek believers. He also desired to stimulate unbelieving Greeks to consider the claims that Jesus Christ is the Perfect Man—the Son of Man—who came in sacrificial service to seek and save sinful mankind. It is evident from the opening lines of this third Gospel that it is addressed to a man named Theophilus. Its purpose was to give Theophilus—and readers today—an accurate historical account of the unique life of Jesus.

Interesting Facts About the Gospel of Luke

▶ It is the most comprehensive Gospel.

▶ It presents all the events of Jesus' life in chronological order.

▶ It is often referred to as the Gospel to Gentiles.

John

Theme: *Jesus Is the Son of God*

John, the writer of the Gospel of John, was an old man when he wrote his account of the life of Christ. He provided a supplement to what had already been written in the first three Gospel accounts. He presented the most powerful and direct case for deity and humanity to be embodied in the Son of God. John showed that in Jesus, perfect humanity and deity are blended, making Jesus the only possible and worthy sacrifice for the sins of mankind.

Eight Signs of Jesus' Divine Nature

1. Turning water to wine — John 2:1-11
2. Healing a nobleman's son — John 4:46-54
3. Healing a cripple at Bethesda — John 5:1-9
4. Feeding 5000 with five loaves and two fish — John 6:1-14
5. Walking on water — John 6:15-21
6. Restoring sight to a blind man — John 9:1-41
7. Raising Lazarus from the dead — John 11:1-44
8. Giving the disciples a large catch of fish — John 21:1-14[8]

"These are written that you may believe that Jesus is the Christ, the Son of God, and that believing you may have life in His name" (JOHN 20:31).

Grace

Grace is unmerited favor. In other words, it is getting something that is undeserved. Grace cannot be earned—it is freely given by God.

Why do we need grace? When Adam disobeyed God in the Garden of Eden, sin entered the world, which produced spiritual death. And because everyone sins, death spread to everyone. There are no religious works a person can do to earn a place in heaven because all are sinners and are unable to pay the debt for sins. But God, in His grace, did what no man could do—He sent His Son, the Lord Jesus, the perfect sacrifice, to die in our place as payment for our debt, and to offer us this grace. (See Romans 5:12; Ephesians 2:8-9.)

> "In Him we have redemption through His blood, the forgiveness of sins, according to the riches of His grace which He made to abound toward us in all wisdom and prudence"
>
> (EPHESIANS 1:7-8).

Greece

After the conquests and subsequent death of Alexander the Great, his entire kingdom was divided among his four generals, just as Daniel had prophesied several hundred years earlier. Through all that, most of the known world came under the influence of Greek culture. By New Testament times Greece was no longer a world power, but it was an extremely influential nation. Paul passed through Greece three times on his missionary journeys. As a result, people in Greece heard the gospel of Jesus Christ, responded to it, and churches were established. (See Daniel 8:2-8,21.)

Alexander the Great

Alexander (whose name means "man-defender") the Great, the son of King Philip of Macedon, was born in 356 B.C. After his father died when he was only 20, Alexander was chosen by the Greeks to be their general in their fight against the Persians, and he went on to conquer almost all of Asia Minor. He was best known for spreading Greek (Hellenistic) culture all over the Near East, and he died in Babylon of a fever in 323 B.C. at only 33 years of age. The prophet Daniel (writing in about 530 B.C.) predicted Alexander's conquest of Persia (330 B.C.) in Daniel 8:3-8,21.

H

Hallelujah

Hallelujah is a transliteration of the Hebrew phrase *hallelu yah,* meaning "praise Yah," or "Praise the Lord." This phrase is used often in the book of Psalms and four times in the New Testament in Revelation 19, where the occupants in heaven are praising God for His work during the end times. (See Revelation 19:1,3,4,6.)

"Praise the Lord!"
Lessons in Praise from Psalms 146–150

The last five psalms in the book of Psalms overflow with praise. Each begins and ends with "Praise the Lord!" They show us where, why, and how to praise God. What does praise do?

1. Praise takes our mind off our problems and shortcomings and helps us focus on God.
2. Praise leads us from individual meditation to corporate worship.
3. Praise causes us to consider and appreciate God's character.
4. Praise lifts our perspective from the earthly to the heavenly.[9]

Heaven

In the Bible, the phrase "the heavens and the earth" describes the entire universe, as in Genesis 1:1. According to biblical understanding, there are three heavens. The first two are visible, and the third is invisible.

- *First heaven.* The first heaven is the sky, or heavens, also referred to as firmament or expanse. (See Genesis 2:19.)

- *Second heaven.* The second heaven is that of the sun, moon, and stars. It refers to all the celestial bodies. One day this heaven, the physical universe, will be destroyed and replaced by God with a new heaven and earth. (See Deuteronomy 17:3; 2 Peter 3:10-13.)

- *Third heaven.* The third heaven is the domain of God. The apostle Paul wrote to the Corinthians about a man (probably himself) who was caught up to the third heaven. After His resurrection, Jesus went up into heaven. He is now preparing a place in heaven for believers and will return for them. (See 2 Corinthians 12:2; Mark 16:19; John 14:2.)

Hebrew Calendar

The Hebrew calendar differs significantly from the Gregorian one. It was how the biblical writers dated events:

Name	Month	Equivalent to...
Nisan (Abib)	1	March–April
Iyar (Ziv)	2	April–May
Sivan	3	May–June
Tammuz	4	June–July
Av	5	July–August
Elul	6	August–September

Name	Month	Equivalent to...
Tishri (Ethanim)	7	September–October
Cheshvan (Bul)	8	October–November
Kislev	9	November–December
Tevet	10	December–January
Shevat	11	January–February
Adar[10]	12	February–March

Hell

The English term *hell* is often used to translate the New Testament term *Gehenna*, which was used in reference to the Valley of Hinnom, an actual geographic region in Jerusalem where refuse and garbage were continually burned. Jesus used the imagery of fire many times when He contrasted Gehenna with the glorious kingdom of God. Hell is a place of judgment and torment for all who have sinned and not placed their trust in the saving work of Jesus on the cross. Its inhabitants suffer darkness, weeping, wailing, gnashing of teeth, and eternal separation from God. (See Matthew 5:22.)

Herod the Great

Rome established Herod the Great as a puppet king who ruled the Jewish people in Palestine from 40 to 4 B.C. He was hated by his Jewish subjects even though he did many things—such as rebuilding the temple—in hopes of appeasing the Jews.

Herod was a cunning leader and true ally of Rome. His many personal family problems led him to murder his wife and two sons. (It was said of him, "It's better to be Herod's hog than Herod's son.") The book of Matthew tells us that Joseph, Jesus' father on earth and

Mary's husband, was warned in a dream that Herod wanted to kill Jesus because he saw Him as a threat to his throne. So Joseph took Mary and the young boy Jesus to Egypt, and they did not return until after Herod's slaughter of innocent children in Bethlehem and Herod's death (Matthew 2:1-21).

Hezekiah

Hezekiah, whose name means "strength of Yahweh" or "strength of God," was one of the kings of the southern kingdom of Judah. Unlike his father, Hezekiah was a righteous king. In 2 Kings 18:5 he was commended for his faithfulness to God. Hezekiah was perhaps most well known for his prayers. In one of his prayers Hezekiah asked God to intervene against an invading Assyrian army. God answered Hezekiah's prayer by killing 185,000 men in the Assyrian camp, causing the Assyrian King Sennacherib to flee. In another prayer, Hezekiah asked God to intervene in his terminal illness. God answered this prayer of devotion and granted Hezekiah an additional 15 years of life. (For Hezekiah's story, see 2 Kings 18:1–20:21.)

A Life Lesson from Hezekiah

You Can Make a Difference!

Is it heredity or environment that shapes your destiny? Hezekiah defied both. His father, Ahaz, was an idolater and closed the temple and placed idols for pagan worship everywhere. Yet Hezekiah's faith and character stands in sharp contrast to that of his father and the spiritual condition of the land. He was one of very few kings in Judah's history whom God compares favorably with King David. During his reign, Hezekiah brought about major spiritual reformation.

You might be asking, "How can I make a difference? I'm just one insignificant person!" Like Hezekiah, you have the weapon of prayer.

Prayer makes a difference. Also, like Hezekiah, you have the powerful weapon of your character. Your godly character will shine light to a dark world. Thank God that He's given you incredible resources so you can make a difference!

Holy Spirit

The Holy Spirit is one of three persons who make up what is commonly referred to as the Trinity. The Trinity is made up of God the Father, God the Son, and God the Holy Spirit. The Holy Spirit is "the Helper" Jesus said He would send after His departure from earth. The Holy Spirit came upon the apostles in Acts 2, and indwells all believers. And it was the Holy Spirit who spoke God's Word through holy men of God. (See John 15:26; 1 Corinthians 6:19; 2 Peter 1:21.)

A Few Facts About the Holy Spirit

▶ Every believer in Christ receives the Holy Spirit (1 Corinthians 12:13).

▶ Every believer in Christ receives spiritual "gifts" from the Holy Spirit for ministry (1 Corinthians 12:7).

▶ Believers are Christlike when they are controlled by the Holy Spirit (Galatians 5:22-23).

▶ Believers are exhorted to walk by the Spirit (Galatians 5:16).

▶ Believers are exhorted not to grieve the Holy Spirit (Ephesians 4:30).

▶ Believers are exhorted not to quench or stifle the Holy Spirit (1 Thessalonians 5:19).

I

Immanuel

The title "Immanuel" is found in the Bible in a promise God made to King Ahaz and the entire house of David through the prophet Isaiah. The term means "God with us." Matthew 1:23 confirms Jesus' birth as the fulfillment of God's promise because Jesus is literally Immanuel, God in the flesh—"God with us." Today, through the Holy Spirit, God is with those who believe in Christ. (See Isaiah 7:14; Matthew 1:23.)

Isaac

Isaac, meaning "he laughs," was the promised and long-awaited son of Abraham and Sarah in the Old Testament. The high point in his life came when he trusted God and his father when he was offered to God as a sacrifice. He married Rebekah, who came from his father's homeland, Mesopotamia. They had twin sons, Esau and Jacob. His low point came when, like his father Abraham, he asked Rebekah to lie about their marital relationship. His cowardice was discovered and he was asked to leave the area by the king of the Philistines.

Isaac is significant in that he is a transitional figure. The promise made by God to Abraham to make Abraham a great nation was passed down to Isaac, who would pass that inheritance down to his son, Jacob. Isaac appears to have been a passive person who took no bold actions. He was content to live in the Promised Land, tending his flocks and herds. Isaac lived 180 years. (For Isaac's story, read Genesis 21–27.)

A Life Lesson from Isaac

Stand for What You Believe

Isaac's quiet spirit was seen early when he offered no objection as his father, Abraham, raised a knife to slay him. This same spirit was again seen in his refusal to be provoked when his enemies claimed his water wells as their own. But Isaac's passive nature had its dark side, which became evident when he refused to defend his wife against the possibility of defilement.

In Matthew 5:9, the Bible speaks of the blessings of being a peacemaker. However, this quality is never to be at the expense of your character, your responsibilities, or your obedience to God's standards. Stand up for what you believe, and trust God to protect your interests and honor your courage.

Isaiah

The prophet Isaiah received from God, in a vision, his commission to prophesy to the people in the southern kingdom of Judah. God appeared to Isaiah in such overwhelming glory that Isaiah's sin became plain to him and he thought he was going to die because he had seen God. But an angel touched Isaiah's mouth with a burning coal and told him that his sin was forgiven.

Isaiah's prophetic ministry spanned the reigns of four kings of Judah—Uzziah, Jotham, Ahaz, and Hezekiah. God used Isaiah to prophesy many things, including the birth of Jesus and His death on behalf of mankind. The book of his prophecies is named after him and has the greatest number of chapters in the Old Testament—66. Isaiah is considered one of the major prophets (the others being Jeremiah, Ezekiel, and Daniel). (See Isaiah 52:13–53:12; 7:14.)

Did you know...?

- Isaiah is considered by many to be the greatest Old Testament prophet.

- Isaiah is quoted some 50 times in the New Testament.

- Isaiah was able to preach the forgiveness of God because he had experienced the forgiveness of God.

- Isaiah's message is divided into 39 chapters about God's judgment followed by 27 chapters about God's grace.

- Isaiah shows you how to follow God even when there is little response from those around you.

Dialogue Between God and Isaiah

God asked: "Whom shall I send, and who will go for Us?"

Isaiah answered: "Here am I! Send me."

(See Isaiah 6:8.)

Israel

Israel (meaning "one who has power with God") is the name God gave to Jacob (see *Jacob*), the son of Isaac. *Israel* also refers to the nation and people who came from Jacob. It was out of Israel that the Messiah eventually came. The Messiah was Jesus, who would not only redeem Israel, but make it possible for all others to have a relationship with God. In Israel's early history, God told the people that He did not choose them because they were the greatest in number. Indeed, they were the fewest of all peoples. No, God chose them because He loved them and would keep the oath He swore to their forefathers. (See Deuteronomy 7:7.)

J

Jacob

Jacob (whose name means "trickster," "heel-grabber," or "supplanter") was a twin born to Isaac and Rebekah. Jacob spent his youth living as a nomad in the land of Canaan with his parents and his older twin brother, Esau. But rivalry between the twins and deception toward his father forced Jacob to flee to Rebekah's family for safety. While he was away, he married two wives and had two concubines, all of whom gave him a total of 12 children.

After many years away from his parents and his brother Esau, Jacob returned to the land of his father. The night before Jacob confronted his brother, who was traveling to meet him, Jacob experienced a unique, nightlong wrestling match with a "man" whom Jacob identified as God in human form. Jacob refused to release his hold on his divine opponent until the Lord blessed him. The Lord then gave him a new name—*Israel*—meaning "he struggles with God." Jacob's 12 children formed the 12 tribes that made up the Jewish nation of Israel, which was named after their father. (For Jacob's story, see Genesis 25–50.)

Jacob's Four Encounters with God

Encounter 1 After Jacob deceived his family and left his home to save himself from his brother Esau's revenge, God appeared to Jacob to confirm His blessing and reveal Himself to Jacob. It was in this encounter that the story of "Jacob's ladder" occurred.

Encounter 2 After Jacob was deceived by his family—by Laban, his father-in-law—God appeared to Jacob and approved of his desire to leave his father-in-law's land and return home.

Encounter 3 On his trip to his homeland, Jacob wrestled with God, grabbing onto God and refusing to let go until God blessed him, which He did.

Encounter 4 After Jacob arrived home, God reminded him of his new name—*Israel*, meaning "one who struggles with God."[11]

A Life Lesson from Jacob

The Soil for Growth

Jacob was certainly not the perfect role model. In his earlier life he had a pronounced tendency to lie, deceive, manipulate, and take matters into his own hands. But things began to change. As Jacob was forced out of his safe environment by his own deception, and was himself lied to and deceived, he began to seek God's provision. By the end of his life, Jacob was unwilling to do anything without asking for God's direction. Because there was such a dramatic transformation in Jacob's heart, God changed Jacob's name from "deceiver" to *Israel*, meaning "God fighter" or "he struggles with God." (See Genesis 32:28.)

As in the case of Jacob, our failures and adversities become the soil for growth. Jacob's misfortunes forced him to trust God. Are you experiencing a time of hardship? Rather than seeing your misfortune as a negative, view your present situation as an opportunity to trust God and grow spiritually. God wants you to learn from your present problem, not to avoid or resent it. Embrace your life as it is with all its trials. Allow God to strengthen you and give you His victory.

The Birth Order of Jacob's 12 Sons

Mother	Son
Leah (wife)	Reuben
	Simeon
	Levi
	Judah
Bilhah (Rachel's maid)	Dan
	Naphtali
Zilpah (Leah's maid)	Gad
	Asher
Leah	Issachar
	Zebulun
Rachel (wife)	Joseph
	Benjamin

Jeremiah

Jeremiah (whose name means "appointed of God") was a man in the village of Anathoth, located just north of Jerusalem in the southern kingdom of Judah. God set Jeremiah apart at birth to be His prophetic mouthpiece.

Jeremiah faithfully communicated God's words to His people for 40 years, warning them about the doom and captivity that was sure to come unless they repented and turned to God. But no one listened to him. Referred to by many Bible teachers as "the weeping prophet," Jeremiah sometimes lost hope regarding the position God had given him. Even the people in his own city hated him. His messages were definitely not popular. But Jeremiah remained obedient to his calling to warn the people. Even in his despair, he praised God. Near the time of God's judgment, Jeremiah stood in the court of the temple of the Lord and proclaimed God's judgment upon Jerusalem and all the surrounding towns because they refused to listen to God's words. The priest and chief officer of the temple responded by hitting Jeremiah and putting him in stocks. Jeremiah's predictions soon became reality as Jerusalem was destroyed and the people were taken into captivity. Jeremiah is also the author of the book of Lamentations, which mourns for the people of God because of their sins. (See Jeremiah 20:1-18; 19:15.)

Jeremiah's messages were not always filled with God's wrath. Often he gave uplifting messages, such as God's declaration that after a time of judgment, He would restore Israel and Judah and establish a new covenant with Israel. (See Jeremiah 29:10-11; 30–31).

A Life Lesson from Jeremiah

Staying on Task

Jeremiah was incredibly obedient to God, even though he suffered immensely for it. His commitment to God was long-term, to the end. Against all odds, he stayed on task, preaching and warning God's people. And the cost of such commitment?

He preached...and the people remained numb or ignored him.

He preached...and the people hated and threatened him.

He preached...and the people whipped and imprisoned him.

Yet Jeremiah refused to waver from God's assignment. He endured in spite of the difficulties. He preached on, even with no response. Yet God faithfully and continually encouraged His prophet. Like Jeremiah, whatever ministry God has given you, don't balk, fall back, or bail.

Turn to God. Review and renew your commitment. Use all God's available resources. Count on His grace to see you through. Like Jeremiah, keep your heart and mind fixed on Him and "Praise the LORD!" (Jeremiah 20:13).

Jerusalem

Originally known as Salem (Hebrew=*shalem*, meaning "peace"), Jerusalem (meaning "foundation of peace") was chosen by the Lord as a central place of His attention. Jerusalem is first mentioned in Genesis 14:19 when Abraham honored its priest—Melchizedek, king of Salem—as a servant of God Most High. The city itself is over 2000 feet above sea level, making it one of the higher-elevation towns in Israel.

Around 1000 B.C., David captured the city and made it the capital of his kingdom, known as the City of David. David made plans to build a temple to God in Jerusalem, but ultimately his son, Solomon, would build it, making Jerusalem the center of worship for all of Israel.

Jesus frequently went up to Jerusalem during His earthly life. Ultimately Jesus was executed on the cross and rose from the dead in Jerusalem. He went up into heaven from Jerusalem, and it is in Jerusalem that He will return in glory and set up His earthly kingdom, where He will rule for 1000 years. Afterward, as part of God's eternal kingdom of a new heaven and earth, a New Jerusalem—having the glory of God—will come down from heaven. (See 1 Kings 14:21; Acts 1:7-11; Revelation 21–22.)

Jesus

Jesus is the greatest man who ever lived. Matthew 1:1 says Jesus is "the Messiah, the son of David, the son of Abraham" (NASB). Jesus was born to a virgin named Mary, who was betrothed (engaged) to Joseph.

An angel commanded Joseph to call Mary's child *Jesus*, an English translation of the Greek *Iesous*, which comes from the Hebrew name *Yeshua*, meaning "the Lord is salvation" or "Savior" because He would save His people from their sins. Jesus, equal to God, came down to earth to dwell among men and become the sinless sacrifice that would deliver those who believe in Him from their sin. (See Matthew 1:1,18-25; John 1:1-14.)

Jesus began His three-year ministry when he was about 30 years old. During this time, He performed many miraculous acts of healing and often demonstrated His power over the forces of nature and the spiritual realm. He taught in the synagogues throughout the regions of Judea and Galilee. Jesus taught that He was the only way to God, the Father, and claimed to be God Himself. The Jewish religious leaders were often upset with His statements and deeds, particularly when He claimed to be God. Sometimes Jesus would draw large crowds and get into debates with the Jewish leaders (see *Pharisees* and *Sadducees*). (See Luke 3:23; John 8:58; 14:6.)

Jesus often communicated His teachings through parables—stories about everyday occurrences that held important meanings (see *Parables*). He also taught through sermons. The Sermon on the Mount, found in Matthew 5–7, is one of Jesus' most famous speeches. In it He...

- refuted misinterpretations of the Hebrew Scriptures and pointed out what they truly mean;

- taught that we ought to love our enemies and pray for those who persecute us;

- gave His followers an example of how to pray in what is popularly known as the Lord's Prayer; and

- instructed us to do to others what we would want others to do to us, which people often refer to as the Golden Rule. (See Matthew 5:44; 6:9-13; 7:12.)

One vital thing Jesus did was to make disciples (see *Disciples, Twelve*).

He chose 12 men to be with Him, to watch Him, to dialogue with Him, and to serve others. Before His ascension into heaven, Jesus issued what is today known as the Great Commission and sent His disciples into the world in His place to make other disciples by teaching them about Him and baptizing them. (See Matthew 10:1-4; 28:19-20.)

Jesus always knew that He was going to die. In fact, He told His disciples early on that this would happen. They did not really understand what He meant until after Jesus' resurrection. The religious leaders hatched a plot to kill Jesus, and, working with Judas Iscariot, one of Jesus' disciples, they succeeded in arresting Him and having Him put to death. (See Mark 8:31.)

Jesus predicted or hinted at His eventual resurrection (see *Resurrection*). Indeed, three days after His crucifixion, Jesus rose from the dead, just as He said He would. The women who had followed Jesus were the first to discover the empty tomb. Angels announced His resurrection. Jesus appeared to Mary and the disciples, and Paul later recorded that Jesus appeared to over 500 people. Paul preached that if Christ had not been raised, our faith would be "empty." (See 1 Corinthians 15:6,14.)

Key Prophecies Jesus Fulfilled at His First Coming

	Old Testament Prophecy	New Testament Fulfillment
Birth in Bethlehem	Micah 5:2	Matthew 2:1-6
Born of a virgin	Isaiah 7:14	Luke 1:26-38
Triumphal entry into Jerusalem	Zechariah 9:9	John 12:12-16
Betrayal by one of His own	Psalm 41:9	Luke 22:19-23,47-48
Silent when accused	Isaiah 53:7	Matthew 27:12-14

Beaten and spit upon	Isaiah 50:6	Matthew 26:67
Death by crucifixion	Zechariah 12:10	John 19:18,37
Will arise and conquer death	Psalm 16:10	Matthew 28:7-10

A Bare Bones Look at Jesus' Life and Ministry

4 B.C.	Birth in Bethlehem	Matthew 2:1
A.D. 26	Baptism and beginning of ministry	Matthew 3:13-17
A.D. 27	First Passover	John 2:13
A.D. 28	Second Passover	John 5:1
A.D. 29	Third Passover	John 6:4
A.D. 30	Fourth Passover (the Last Supper)	John 12:1-12
	The crucifixion	Luke 23:26-49
	The resurrection	John 20:1-18
	The ascension	Acts 1:9-11

A Life Lesson from Jesus

Impacting the World

How was it possible for Jesus to have such a colossal impact on the world when He lived for only 33 years and taught for a short three years in one small area of the world, an area that measured a mere 44 miles long and 25 miles wide? The answer? Discipleship. Jesus took a small band of 12 ordinary men and in three years trained and turned them into a force that shook the very foundations of the world. They were empowered by God's Spirit and took the message of Jesus' resurrection and His offer of forgiveness for sin to the ends of the earth.

Do you want to impact the world? Then discipleship must be key in your life as well. First, be His disciple. Ensure that His message and conduct take control of you. Follow Him without flinching. Extend His forgiveness to others. Live in a way that draws others to Him. Then be available to spend time with others who also desire to be Jesus' disciples. Wherever you live and work, you can have an impact. Speak of the Lord. Invite others to church. Spend time and form friendships. Teach those who want to learn more. And help them with their ministries.

A Prayer to Pray

Lord, please empower me as You did those early disciples so that I too can shake the very foundations of my world. Amen.

Who Is Jesus?

The Seven "I Ams" of Jesus

I am the bread of life .... John 6:35,48

I am the light of the world .... John 8:12; 9:5

I am the door .... John 10:7,9

I am the good shepherd .... John 10:11,14

I am the resurrection and the life .... John 11:25

I am the way, the truth, and the life .... John 14:6

I am the true vine .... John 15:1,5

Jew

The English word *Jew* comes from *Judah*, one of the 12 sons of

Jacob (see *Tribes of Israel, Twelve*). The term *Jew* (at least on an ethnic level) first shows up in the Old Testament after the deportation of the Israelites to Babylon. A Jew became synonymous with anyone who was descended from Abraham, Isaac, and Jacob or who followed the religion of Judaism, a term also derived from *Judah*. Why are the Jews so important? God told Abraham that in his seed, or descendants, all the nations of the earth would be blessed. God chose Israel from among the nations to bring forth His Son, Jesus, a Jew, to die so that salvation could come not just to Jews, but to everyone. (See 2 Kings 25:25; Genesis 22:18.)

Did you know...?

The Jews are often referred to as "the apple of God's eye"
(see Zechariah 2:8).

Job

Job lived in the land of Uz and was described by God as blameless and upright, one who feared God and avoided evil. He had seven sons, three daughters, and was extremely wealthy *and* extremely faithful to God. (See Job 1:1.)

One day Satan came before God and accused Job of being upright and wealthy only because of God's goodness and blessings. To these accusations, God replied that His servant Job was righteous and there was no one on earth like him. Satan then claimed that Job would turn away from God and curse Him if God took away everything that Job had. God allowed Satan to do what he willed with Job, and Job lost all his children, as well as his servants and livestock. But Job still praised and blessed God. Satan tried again to get Job to curse God by striking Job with painful boils. Amazingly, Job responded positively to that as well, even when his wife tried to get him to curse God. (See Job 1:6,8,11,21.)

In addition to the charges Satan brought against Job, three of Job's friends accused him of having done something wrong and being punished by God. But God Himself scolded Job's friends and answered their false accusations. Through all the incriminations, Job proved to be genuinely righteous and faithful, and in the end God blessed him even more than before. (See Job 42:12-16. For Job's story, see the book of Job, especially chapters 1 and 42.)

A Life Lesson from Job

Suffering to the Glory of God

Suffering is a fact of life. Since Adam and Eve introduced sin into the world, trials, trauma, tragedy, and tribulation have become familiar daily realities. But, like Job, you can suffer to the glory of God. When hard times show up on your doorstep, stay faithful to God. Continue to love Him, serve Him, and trust Him. Like Job, be unwavering in your walk with God. Do what is right. Praise God with your lips. Humble yourself before Him. Believe that He is in constant control... no matter what. As you remain faithful in your suffering, God is honored and glorified.

"Beloved, do not think it strange concerning the fiery trial which is to try you, as though some strange thing happened to you; but rejoice to the extent that you partake of Christ's sufferings, that when His glory is revealed, you may also be glad with exceeding joy"

(1 PETER 4:12-13).

John the Baptist

John the Baptist (whose story is told in all four gospels and predicted by two Old Testament prophets) was the son of a priest named Zacharias and his wife, Elizabeth, who was related to Mary, the mother of Jesus. John was a fiery, passionate preacher who wore a garment of camel's hair and ate locusts and wild honey. His mission was to prepare the way for the Messiah, Jesus. He thought of himself as only a "voice" calling people to repentance. When they responded, he baptized them by immersing them in the Jordan River. He even baptized Jesus, which at first he was reluctant to do. Jesus called John the last and greatest of the prophets. Ultimately John was beheaded at the age of 30 by King Herod at the insistence of his wife, Herodias. His ministry lasted only about one year. (See Luke 1:36; Matthew 3:1-15; 11:11; 14:6-11.)

A Life Lesson from John the Baptist

How Important Is One Year of Life?

Have you ever thought to yourself, *I have lots of time for...*(and you can fill in the blank)? Well, what if John the Baptist had had that kind of blasé mentality about his time and days? I'm sure John didn't know that his ministry would last only one brief year, but he made sure to make his time count for God.

How important is this next year of your life? What if you were told you had only one year to live? How would you spend that priceless year? I'm sure you might make a few changes in your life, right? Why not set a one-year goal, starting today? Then break down that goal to what you must do month by month, and finally to what you must do today to make your day and your year—and your life—count toward God's plan for your life, your loved ones, and His purposes for mankind.

Jonah

Jonah is the name of a prophet of God, and also the book of the

Bible that tells his story is named after him. This book spotlights the love of God—He called upon the prophet Jonah to go to Nineveh and warn the people there of coming judgment. But Jonah got on a ship and fled to Tarshish, which was in the opposite direction of Nineveh. While sailing to Tarshish, the boat carrying Jonah encountered a terrible storm, and the ship was about to break apart. The sailors were frightened for their lives and cried out to their gods. When it became known that Jonah was the cause of the stormy seas, he was thrown overboard. God then sent a "great fish," which swallowed Jonah. He remained in the belly of the fish for three days and nights. Jonah repented of his sin, and the fish spat Jonah out on dry land. God again commanded Jonah to go to Nineveh, and this time Jonah complied. Upon arriving at the city, he warned its inhabitants of impending doom. The people of Nineveh repented, turned to God, and God spared them. (See Jonah 1:4,7; 3:10.)

Jonah should have been deliriously happy, but he was angry. He did not want God to forgive the Ninevites because they had been such an evil people. As Jonah brooded in the hot sun, God provided a plant to shade him, and then sent a worm to eat the plant. When Jonah responded in anger at the loss of the plant and its shade, God pointed out to Jonah that he had shown more concern about a plant than he had for the 120,000 people of Nineveh. (See Jonah 4.)

A Life Lesson from Jonah

Learning More About God's Love

God responds to the prayers of those who call on Him.

He spared the lives of the sailors on the ship to Tarshish when they pleaded for mercy.

He spared Jonah when he prayed from inside the fish.

He spared Nineveh when the people responded to Jonah's preaching.

God gives second chances.

He sent His prophet Jonah to Nineveh to give the people a chance to repent and be saved.

He patiently waited and gave Jonah a second chance to serve Him and save others.

God loves all the people of the world.

He used Jonah as an object lesson to show His love and compassion for all His creation—even Israel's enemy, Assyria, of which Nineveh was the capital city.[12]

Jordan River

The Jordan River descends from Mount Hermon (1200 feet above sea level) in northern Israel, flows through the Sea of Galilee, and ends in the south at the Dead Sea, traveling a distance of 250 miles. When it flows into the Dead Sea (or Salt Sea), the Jordan River reaches the lowest elevation of any river on earth—1290 feet below sea level. In Bible times, the Jordan was known for it fertile banks. Joshua and the people of Israel crossed it to conquer the land of Canaan. The Jordan was also the site of two other famous crossings—Elijah and Elisha miraculously crossed it on dry ground. It was the river in which Naaman was dipped and healed of his leprosy, and it was where John the Baptist baptized Jesus. Today the Jordan River is the border between the nations of Israel and Jordan. (See Joshua 3:15-17; 2 Kings 2:8,14; 5:14; Mark 1:9.)

The Jordan River

Joshua

Joshua (whose name means "Yahweh is salvation") was the son of
Nun and is first mentioned in Exodus 17:9 as receiving orders from
Moses to organize an army against the Amalekites. He was Moses'

servant or assistant. Joshua was also one of the 12 spies Moses sent into the Promised Land to bring back information about the land and its people. Joshua and Caleb were the only two spies who brought back a positive report. Therefore they were the only ones of the 12 spies permitted to later enter the land of Canaan because of their trust in God to give them victory over the Canaanites.

After Moses died, Joshua became his successor and led the people of Israel on military campaigns throughout Canaan, eventually conquering the entire land and dividing it up. Before he died, Joshua urged the people of Israel to serve God alone. The people responded in the affirmative and Joshua held them to their oath. They served God faithfully during the rest of Joshua's life.

Joshua is also the name of the Old Testament book that describes Joshua's leadership and the exploits of the Israelites as they, together with God, conquered a land and people who were stronger, more numerous, and who lived in walled cities.

A Life Lesson from Joshua

Going the Distance

Joshua was a faithful servant of Moses, and when the time came, he faithfully served God as commander of all the Israelite forces. He was committed to obeying God fully, and he was devoted to ensuring that the people followed God all the days of his life. When their faithfulness faltered, Joshua gave a challenge to the people to follow his example. He said, "As for me and my house, we will serve the LORD" (Joshua 24:15). Not one negative word is recorded in the Bible about this servant of both God and Moses.

How would you rate your faithfulness both to your earthly leaders and your heavenly Father? Commitment is not a sprint race. It's a lifelong marathon! Ask God to give you the endurance to go the distance in your commitments to your family, your church, your job, and especially to your Lord.

Judah, Kingdom of

Judah originally was a tribal territory in the southern part of the nation of Israel. However, ten of the twelve tribes of Israel revolted against King Rehoboam (the grandson of David, who was from the tribe of Judah) because he said he would increase the burdens of taxes and compulsory labor, which his father, Solomon, had inflicted on them. Only the tribes of Judah and Benjamin remained loyal to the house of David, and they constituted the southern kingdom of Judah. Being that Jesus came from the line of David, He was a descendant from Judah.

The northern kingdom of Israel was established under Jeroboam, who led Israel astray with the worship of two golden calves he set up in the tribal cities of Dan and Bethel. This encouraged Israel to disobey God and worship in places other than at Jerusalem.

Judges

Judges is the name of one of the historical books of the Old Testament as well as the name of a group of Bible characters. After Joshua's death (see *Joshua*), the people of Israel quickly turned to idols, provoking God to anger. He then judged them through Israel's enemies, who plundered and oppressed them. When the people cried out to God for help, He would appoint a judge to deliver the people from their oppressors. But once a judge died, the people of Israel would go right back to their wicked ways. God would then allow enemy nations to oppress Israel again. This cycle of oppression and deliverance was repeated several times. (See Judges 2:16-23.)

The Judges	*versus*	Their Enemies
Othniel		The Mesopotamians
Ehud		The Moabites and Ammonites

Shamgar . . . . The Philistines

Deborah . . . . The Canaanites

Gideon . . . . The Midianites

Tola and Jair . . . . The evil of Abimelech

Jephthah, Ibzan, Elon, Abdon . . . . The Ammonites

Samson . . . . The Philistines

K

Kingdom of God/Heaven

Only Matthew uses the expression "Kingdom of Heaven" out of sensitivity to his Jewish readers (Matthew 3:2; 4:17; 5:3, for example). The rest of Scripture uses "the kingdom of God." Both expressions refer to the sphere of God's rule over those who belong to Him. The kingdom is now manifest in heaven's spiritual rule over the hearts of believers. When Jesus returns, this kingdom will be established as a literal, earthly kingdom. (See Luke 17:21; Revelation 20:4-6.)

About the Kingdom of God

Jesus:

...said that it was near	Mark 1:15
...taught that it was very difficult to enter	Mark 10:24
...explained that unless one is born again he cannot enter	John 3:5

Paul:

...wrote that the unrighteous would not inherit this kingdom	1 Corinthians 6:9
...called a group of disciples "fellow workers" for this kingdom	Colossians 4:11
...taught that those who suffer are worthy of this kingdom	2 Thessalonians 1:5

Kings of the North (Israel) and South (Judah)

After the reign of King Solomon, the nation of Israel split into two kingdoms. These are the kings of the northern and southern kingdoms, beginning with the division between Rehoboam, of David's line in Judah, and Jeroboam, a dissident who became the first king of the northern kingdom of Israel:

King of Israel	Length of Reign (B.C.)	Good or Bad?
Jeroboam I	931–911	Bad
Nadab	911–910	Bad
Baasha	910–887	Bad
Elah	887–886	Bad
Zimri	886	Bad
Omri	886–875	Bad
Ahab	875–853	Bad
Ahaziah	853–852	Bad
Joram (Jehoram)	852–841	Bad
Jehu	841–814	Bad
Jehoahaz	814–798	Bad
Joash (Jehoash)	798–782	Bad
Jeroboam II	782–753	Bad
Zechariah	753–752	Bad
Shallum	752	Bad
Menahem	752–742	Bad
Pekahiah	742–740	Bad
Pekah	740–732	Bad
Hoshea	732–722	Bad

King of Judah	Length of Reign (B.C.)	Good or Bad?
Rehoboam	930–915	Bad
Abijam	915–912	Bad
Asa	912–871	Good
Jehoshaphat	871–849	Good
Jehoram (Joram)	849–842	Bad
Ahaziah	842–841	Bad
Athaliah (queen)	841–835	Bad
Joash (Jehoash)	835–796 (started at age 7)	Good
Amaziah	796–767	Good
Uzziah (Azariah)	767–740	Good
Jotham	750–735	Good
Ahaz	735–715	Bad
Hezekiah	715–687	Good
Manasseh	687–642 (started at age 12)	Bad
Amon	642–640	Bad
Josiah	640–609 (started at age 8)	Good
Jehoahaz	609	Bad
Jehoiakim	609–598	Bad
Jehoiachin (Jeconiah)	598–597	Bad
Zedekiah	597–586	Bad

L

Laban

Laban, a wealthy shepherd, was Rebekah's brother, Isaac's brother-in-law, and Jacob's uncle. Laban was also the father of Rachel and Leah. Perhaps Laban is best known for deceiving Jacob into marrying his older daughter, Leah, when Jacob thought he was marrying Rachel. In the end, Jacob married both, for he loved Rachel. Laban's most distinguishing quality is a negative one—he manipulated, tricked, and deceived others for his own benefit. (For Laban's story, see Genesis 27:43–31:55.)

See *Jacob*.

Languages of the Bible

The Bible was written primarily in Hebrew and Greek (and there is also a little Aramaic). It's no accident that the Bible was written in these different languages. Hebrew is a poetic language and ideal for the narrative story of the Old Testament. Greek, however, was the universal language at the time the New Testament was written, which made the Bible a book for all people. Greek is also a very precise language, which ensured that there would be no doubt what God meant about the doctrines communicated in the New Testament.

Hebrew—Most of the Old Testament was originally composed in Hebrew. Hebrew was the language of the ancient Israelites (or Jews), and it is still known and spoken today. Hebrew is read from right to left. It also has no formally written vowels. Around A.D. 900, a group of Jewish scholars, the Masoretes, came up with a vowel point system made up of dots, slashes, and dashes. This system is still used in most biblical texts to this day. Jesus probably spoke and read Hebrew often. He is usually quoted speaking Aramaic, which many scholars believe was His primary spoken language. (For an example, see Mark 5:41.)

Greek—After the establishment of the Greco-Roman Empire, Hellenistic (Greek) culture was so widespread that in order to conduct daily business, everyone had to be able to speak at least common or marketplace Greek, even if it was not their primary language. This is the kind of Greek the New Testament was written in—everyday language.

Law of Moses

The law of Moses, or *torah*, specifically refers to the first five books of the Old Testament. The torah was God's instruction specifically to His people, Israel. The law of Moses contained everything from the Ten Commandments to what to wear and what to eat. Everything spiritual as well as social and physical was included in this law. By the time of Jesus, the Jews had added an elaborate system of "dos and don'ts" to the law that were used to determine a person's standing with God. However, the law—including the Ten Commandments—was not an instrument of salvation. Rather, it was meant to point out sin and the need for a Savior, Jesus Christ the Lord.

Leprosy

Leprosy is a terrible skin disease that causes the victim's skin to rot, and left untreated, it can cause permanent damage. In Bible times, leprosy was often thought to be a horrible punishment from God, and lepers were required to live outside towns and away from people because they were "unclean." Specific instructions were given in Leviticus 13–14 concerning the treatment of lepers, and during His earthly ministry, Jesus healed lepers. (See Leviticus 13:46; Matthew 8:2-4; Luke 17:11-19.)

Levites

The Levites, who were from the Israelite tribe of Levi, assisted the priests. They were direct descendants of Moses' brother Aaron, also from the tribe of Levi (see *Aaron*). They had specific duties in relation to caring for the tabernacle, and later, the temple. The book of Leviticus is named after the Levites because it consists of Levitical instruction.

Lot

When God called Abram to leave his country of birth and go to the land of Canaan, Abram took his nephew Lot along with the rest of his family. Because both Abram and Lot had many flocks, herds, and tents, the new land could not sustain the both of them, which caused conflict between their herdsmen. Abram didn't want this discord to continue between him and his nephew, so he allowed Lot to pick the portion of the land he wanted, while Abram took the rest. Lot settled in Sodom, while Abram stayed in Canaan. Later, because of a war, Lot was taken captive, and Abram went to rescue him. Sometime later a conflict with the men of Sodom and the promised destruction of that city by God's power forced Lot and his family to leave. The family was told not to look back, but Lot's wife did, and she became a pillar of salt. The last thing we hear of Lot is that his own daughters defiled him in an effort to preserve their family line. (For Lot's story, see Genesis 12–19.)

A Life Lesson from Lot

How Not to Make a Decision

Lot and Abram had a good problem. They had both prospered and owned many sheep, cattle, and other livestock. In an effort to reduce the conflict between their two groups, Abram offered a solution. "Lot, look around and then choose a direction. Then I'll go in the opposite direction." Lot did the thing most people do—he chose what looked good. He chose the lush, green valley floor of the Jordan Valley. The only problem was that the two most wicked and sinful cities of that day, Sodom and Gomorrah, were also located in that valley. This decision ultimately cost Lot his possessions, his wife, and the morality of his daughters, a dear price indeed for his decision to choose what looked good!

How about you? What guidelines help shape your decision-making process? Are your choices based on what *looks* good or what *is* good? Do you pray before you make decisions, or do you plow ahead without asking God or godly people for counsel? Every decision is important. Don't fail to include God in your decision making!

M

Magdalene, Mary

Mary Magdalene was called *Magdalene* because she was from the town of Magdala, which was probably on the shore of the Sea of Galilee. She was a follower of Jesus. We know very little about her, but apparently seven demons had come out of her. She was also one of the women at Jesus' empty tomb. John's Gospel is the only one that records her encounter with the risen Jesus, whom she at first mistook for a gardener. She pleaded with the man to please tell her where he had laid Jesus so she could take Him away. At this point Jesus simply said, "Mary!" That's all it took for her to recognize Jesus, who cautioned her not to hold on to Him because He would soon be returning to the Father. (See Luke 8:2; John 20.)

A Life Lesson from Mary Magdalene

Sharing with Others

A good way to share your spiritual story with others is by describing your life before you met Christ, how you met Christ, and how your life has changed since meeting Christ. Here's how Mary Magdalene's story or testimony would flesh out:

Before she met Christ—Mary Magdalene was possessed by seven demons or evil spirits.

How she met Christ—We don't know when or where, but Jesus freed Mary Magdalene from the demons.

How her life changed after meeting Christ—Mary Magdalene

became a devout follower of Jesus, giving and sharing her funds, possessions, and time to support Him and His ministry. It was her complete devotion that moved her to stay with her Savior at the crucifixion and go to His tomb at the first opportunity after He was buried.

Have you met Christ? Perhaps today will be the day of salvation for you, the day you acknowledge your sin and need for a Savior and place your trust in Jesus. And if you have become a child of God through Christ, recall the amazing details of that wonderful day. Then spend time recounting your spiritual growth and the marvelous changes He has graciously orchestrated in your life. Be sure to tell your story to others. Share it with as many as you can! It's too good to keep to yourself.

Marriage

The first "marriage" in the Bible occurred in Genesis 2:24, when God created the man Adam and the woman Eve and brought them together to form a union. His instructions to the first couple were that they become one flesh. While the Bible mentions Middle Eastern customs concerning marriage, it also provides universal principles for all people.

In Bible times, it was common for the father to arrange a marriage for his son. In traditional Jewish marriages, the groom and bride would enjoy a week-long wedding feast at the home of the groom's parents. The parents would bless the bride and groom and offer proof of the bride's virginity. If a Jewish girl betrothed to be married was not a virgin, she could be stoned to death.

Much is written in the Bible about marriage. Here are a few additional facts:

▶ God created marriage between two people—a man and a woman.

▸ One of the Ten Commandments forbids adultery.

▸ Leaders in the church are expected to set an example by being husbands of only one wife.

▸ Scripture commands that husbands love their wives and wives are to love and submit to their husbands.

▸ Neither the husband nor the wife has authority over his or her body—they are mutually responsible to one another.

▸ Marriage is an illustration of Christ and the church.[13]

Mary, Mother of Jesus

Mary, a teenage Jewish girl living in Nazareth, was betrothed to be married to a man named Joseph. It was this virgin girl whom God chose to give birth to His Son, Jesus, who would save the world from its sins.

Mary never expected that she would be the one chosen to bear the Messiah! The angel Gabriel appeared to her one day and told her she had found favor with God and would conceive a child and bring forth a Son to be named Jesus. It was this child who would be called the Son of the Highest. To Him God would give the throne of His father David. He would reign over the house of Jacob forever, and there would be no end to His kingdom. After Mary asked how such a thing could happen to her when she was a virgin, Gabriel explained that the Holy Spirit would come upon her and the power of the Highest would overshadow her. In other words, it would be a miracle. (See Luke 1:30-35.)

When Joseph realized Mary was pregnant, he decided not to shame her publicly (thinking, understandably, that she had been unfaithful to him). Instead, he planned to quietly and privately divorce her. But an angel came to him in a dream and told him to go ahead and take

Mary as his wife, explaining that the child in Mary was conceived of the Holy Spirit. The angel explained that Mary would bring forth a Son to be named *Jesus* (meaning "God saves"), for He would save His people from their sins. So Joseph kept Mary a virgin until she bore Jesus in Bethlehem, where they had gone because of a government census in the land that required people to register in the town of their birth. They placed the newborn baby Jesus in a manger because there was no room for them in the local inn. After shepherds visited Jesus and shared what they had heard about the child, Mary kept all these things in her heart and thought about them. (See Matthew 1:20-21; Luke 2:7,19.)

For about 33 years, Mary watched and witnessed Jesus, the Son of God, grow from infancy to a teacher of truth and the perfect sacrifice for the sins of the world. In the end, when Jesus was hanging on the cross, Jesus entrusted His mother to John, the beloved disciple, for care. After Jesus' ascension into heaven, Jesus' mother was among those praying continually in the upper room. She was the only human who was with Jesus from birth to death. (See John 19:26-27; Acts 1:14.)

> "I am the Lord's servant, and I am willing
> to accept whatever he wants."
>
> —MARY, THE MOTHER OF JESUS (LUKE 1:38 NLT)

A Portrait of the Life of Mary

M—magnified the Lord in verbal praise (Luke 1:46-55)

A—acknowledged God as her Savior (Luke 1:47)

R—remembered all that happened to her and her Son (Luke 2:19)

Y—yearned to obey God, no matter what (Luke 1:38)

Messiah

See *Anointed One.*

Miracles of the Bible

A miracle is an event in which a natural force is countered by a supernatural force. As some say, it's "a God thing." Throughout the Bible miracles had three purposes—to glorify God, confirm God's message, and meet human needs. And we see a variety of miracles recorded. Prophets such as Moses, Elijah, and Elisha all did miracles that were empowered by God. These miracles included the parting of the Red Sea, the healing of leprosy, the resurrection of the dead, and more. Jesus performed many miracles, such as raising Lazarus from the dead, casting out demons, walking on water, healing people from illnesses, turning water into wine, feeding thousands of people with little food, and more, including His own resurrection from the dead. His miracles showed that He had sovereign control over the supernatural, physical, and spiritual realms.

Money of the Bible

Money has always been a major part of society, and that was true in Bible times. Here are a few examples of the kinds of money mentioned in the Bible:

Shekel. A shekel was a weight of gold, silver, or brass consolidated into a coin. Its use was widespread throughout the ancient Middle East. The term comes from the Hebrew word *shaqal,* meaning "to weigh." Today, the currency of Israel is the shekel, but the Israeli new shekel is not to be confused with the kind used in Bible times.

Mina. The mina was the equivalent of 50 shekels. Jesus used minas in His parable of the ten minas, or the parable of the ten talents. A mina was the equivalent of about three months' wages. (See Luke 19:11-27; Matthew 25:14-30.)

Denarius. The denarius was a day's wages in the Roman Empire during the time of Jesus. Mary, the sister of Lazarus, poured a pound of perfume on Jesus' feet that could have been sold for 300 denarii, or 11 months' wages. (See John 12:1-8.)

A Life Lesson Regarding Money

Where's Your Heart?

Jesus said where your treasure is, there your heart will be too. He also said no one can serve both God and money. Money itself is not bad—it's what we choose to do with money that can be bad. The Bible says that the love of money is the root of all kinds of evil, which reminds us that God should be first in our lives. All wealth, possessions, and money belong to God, and we are simply stewards of it.

Here's a good exercise: Look at your last bank statement. How have you been choosing to use your money? Are you choosing to give to your church, to God's work, to those in need, to worthy causes? Make sure you are using God's resources in the best ways. It will reveal where your heart is. (See Matthew 6:21,24; 1 Timothy 6:10.)

Mordecai

Mordecai was Esther's older cousin (see *Esther*), who brought her up as his own daughter after her parents died. After Esther became queen of Persia, Mordecai heard about a plot by a man named Haman (the prime minister of the kingdom) to kill all the Jews. Through a series of events Mordecai, with the assistance of Esther, the queen, foiled the plot. Haman was executed, the Jews were allowed to defend themselves, and Mordecai became the prime minister in Haman's place. (For Mordecai's story, see the book of Esther.)

--- A Life Lesson from Mordecai ---

Being a Positive Influence

Mordecai was a positive influence throughout his life and throughout an entire kingdom. He positively influenced his younger cousin, Esther, by giving her wise counsel. He was instrumental in the overthrow of an evil man intent on killing all God's people. God's final words regarding this faithful man record how he worked for the good of others, encouraged others throughout the kingdom, and represented the welfare of the Jews in the royal court.

Is it your goal to make a positive difference in the lives of others—those whom God has placed in your life? You can make a difference. Use your God-given position, possessions, and opportunities to help others today and every day.

Moses

Moses got his name (which means "drawn out") from Pharaoh's daughter, who gave him this name because she literally drew him out of a basket floating on the waters of the Nile River. Moses was chosen by God to lead the people of Israel out of the land of Egypt and into the land of Canaan, or the Promised Land. Moses' life can be divided into three time periods:

Moses' first 40 years, in Egypt—Moses was born to Amram and Jochebed, descendants of the tribe of Levi. Because of an edict from the Egyptian Pharaoh that all Hebrew baby boys should be killed, Moses' mother placed him in a basket and set it among the reeds by the bank of the Nile in order to hide him. Moses' older sister, Miriam, stood at a distance to see what would happen to him. Soon Pharaoh's daughter came to bathe in the Nile, and when she saw the basket, she ordered a servant to retrieve it. Looking upon the child, she felt compassion for it and realized he was one of the Hebrews' children. Miriam asked Pharaoh's daughter if she could get a nurse from among the Hebrews for the child, and Pharaoh's daughter agreed. In this way, God made it possible for Moses' mother to nurse him until he was old enough to live as the son of Pharaoh's daughter. While in the palace, Moses received the finest education possible. (See Exodus 2:1-10; 6:20.)

When Moses was a grown man, one day he went out to see how his fellow Hebrews worked, and he noticed an Egyptian beating a Hebrew. Moses checked to see if anyone was watching, and proceeded to kill the Egyptian and hide him in the sand. Later, a Hebrew slave told Moses he knew about his murder of the Egyptian, and Moses became afraid. Soon Pharaoh heard about what had happened, and he wanted to kill Moses. So Moses fled to Midian.

Moses' second 40 years, in Midian—Moses stayed in the desert for 40 years as a shepherd. While there he took a wife named Zipporah, and they had two sons, named Gershom and Eliezer. After 40 years, God spoke to Moses from a burning bush and told him to go back to Egypt.

Moses' third 40 years, in the wilderness—God called Moses to free the Hebrew people. After initial reluctance, Moses, with the help of Aaron, his brother, went back to Egypt to confront Pharaoh, who was oppressing the children of Israel as slaves. God hardened Pharaoh's heart, and ten plagues (see *Ten Plagues*) were sent from God before Pharaoh finally let the people of Israel go. Moses triumphantly led the Israelites out of Egypt, but Pharaoh soon changed his mind and went after them, seemingly trapping them at the Red Sea. God caused the waters of the Red Sea to part, and Moses and the people of Israel crossed successfully. When the Egyptian army followed, the waters came back down and drowned the Egyptians.

During the Israelites' journey through the wilderness, God gave Moses the Ten Commandments. Along the way, Moses had to deal continually with a "stiff-necked" and disobedient people. When they arrived at the Promised Land, they were to conquer it. But the people failed to trust God and were afraid of the size of the people in the land. God punished the Israelites and condemned them to wander in the wilderness for 40 years. During the wanderings, the disobedient generation of Israelites died off, leaving a new generation to enter the land (along with Joshua and Caleb, who had advised the people to not be afraid of the inhabitants of Canaan).

Moses also was not allowed to enter the Promised Land because of an incident in which God told Moses to speak to a rock to get water for the people, but Moses disobeyed God and struck it instead. God allowed Moses to view the Promised Land from the top of Mount Nebo before he died. (See Deuteronomy 34.)

A Life Lesson from Moses

Going the Distance

Moses was far from perfect, and he didn't always obey God. But God was patient with Moses and used him mightily to communicate His message to Pharaoh and to Israel, even though Moses claimed he was not an able communicator. The book of Deuteronomy closes with a eulogy for Moses, testifying that there was never again a prophet like Moses in Israel. (See Exodus 4:10; Deuteronomy 34:10-12.)

In the end, when all is said and done, what's important about your life is faithfulness. It's not how you start, but how you finish that counts. Everyone stumbles, balks, hesitates, fails, and feels unqualified at one time or another. But what matters is going the distance—continuing to follow God, trying to complete the work He gives you, and trusting in His power, might, and grace to see you to the finish line.

Mount of Olives

The Mount of Olives is an important geographical location in Israel. According to Zechariah 14:4, when Christ returns to set up His earthly kingdom, His feet will stand on the Mount of Olives, and He will become king over all the earth. It was also on the Mount of Olives that Jesus delivered His famous Olivet Discourse—that is, He talked about the destruction of the temple in Jerusalem and what would take place in the last days.

Jesus and His disciples went regularly to the Mount of Olives, and they went there shortly before Jesus' betrayal. It was in the Garden of Gethsemane that Jesus prayed, was betrayed by Judas, arrested by soldiers, and taken away to face an unjust trial before His crucifixion. (See Matthew 24–25; 26:36-57.)

Music of the Bible

Throughout the Bible, music is a key element of worship and praise. The first mention of music is in Genesis 4:21, which refers to two musical instruments—the lyre (a U-shaped harp) and the pipe (a common wind instrument). Here is a list of some of the musical instruments used in Bible times.

- The *ram's horn* was a curved ram's horn used during Jewish worship practices. It is mentioned frequently throughout the Hebrew Bible. This instrument emits a loud blast.

- The *lyre* (or harp) was a common string instrument in the ancient world. It is the instrument David played to soothe King Saul.

- The *pipe* was a common wind instrument in the ancient world and is similar to a flute.

- The *trigon* was a triangular lyre.

▶ The *psaltery* was a bottle-shaped harp. Meant to accompany the voice, it was often used in worship. (See Genesis 4:21; Exodus 19:13,16; 1 Samuel 16:23.)

A Lesson on Worship

Make a Joyful Noise to the Lord

The Bible is filled with music, and the psalms abound with joyful praises involving music. Music is a wonderful tool to use when worshiping God. You can also lift up your voice as an instrument of worship. The psalms declare, "I will sing praises to my God while I have my being...Sing to the LORD with thanksgiving...Sing to the LORD a new song...Let them sing praises to Him" (Psalm 146:2; 147:7; 149:1,3).

Let All Things Praise the Lord
Psalm 150:3-6

Praise Him with the sound of the trumpet;
praise Him with the lute and harp!
Praise Him with the timbrel and dance;
praise Him with stringed instruments and flutes!
Praise Him with loud cymbals;
praise Him with clashing cymbals!
Let everything that has breath praise the LORD.
Praise the LORD!

N

Nebuchadnezzar

Nebuchadnezzar is considered the greatest of the Babylonian kings. In 605, 597, and 586 B.C., King Nebuchadnezzar took large numbers of people from Judah into captivity. Nebuchadnezzar was well known for his many construction projects that made Babylon famous. He even went so far as to build a giant gold image and commanded his government officials of all the conquered peoples to assemble and bow down to it. Shadrach, Meschach, and Abednego, all friends of Daniel (see *Daniel*), refused to bow down to Nebuchadnezzar's statue, so he had them thrown into a fiery furnace. But they were not harmed. (See Daniel 3.)

King Nebuchadnezzar had dreams, which only Daniel could interpret. Concerning the first dream, Daniel told Nebuchadnezzar about powerful kingdoms to come. About the second dream, Daniel told Nebuchadnezzar that God had decreed that the king would live like and with the beasts of the field, which happened to Nebuchadnezzar until he recognized God's supremacy over his finite kingdom. Whatever happened, it is clear from the text that God was humbling Nebuchadnezzar. (See the book of Daniel.)

A Life Lesson from Nebuchadnezzar

Who's in Control?

Nebuchadnezzar was a powerful king who conquered many peoples and built incredible construction projects, including the hanging gardens that are considered to be one of the seven wonders of the ancient world. Yet he had one serious flaw—he was all pride and zero humility! Nebuchadnezzar believed everything he had was a result of his own power and abilities. He never considered God in any of his thinking. It was only after an encounter with God that Nebuchadnezzar finally acknowledged God's sovereign control over all things.

Do you think you are in control of your life and schedule? If you do, learn a lesson from Nebuchadnezzar. Once he was humbled by God because of his pride and arrogance, he acknowledged that God "does according to His will...among the inhabitants of the earth. No one can restrain His hand" (Daniel 4:35). Acknowledge God's control by praying as you plan. Seek His will in all your activities—even the smallest things. Ask for His wisdom in the use of your time and talents. Acknowledging God glorifies God!

Nehemiah

Nehemiah is the name of a book of the Old Testament that tells the adventures of the man Nehemiah. A Jew and cupbearer for the king of Persia, Nehemiah led a small group of people from Babylon back to Jerusalem for the purpose of rebuilding the city's walls. His autobiography describes the great opposition he and his men suffered from the Jews within the city and the hostile forces surrounding the city. Yet Nehemiah and his helpers were able to finish rebuilding the city walls in just 52 days! How was this extraordinary feat accomplished? Nehemiah's story reveals he was highly dependent on God's support. He prayed when he was discouraged, when under attack, and when he felt weak and powerless. This close relationship with God, combined with his leadership and organizational skills, made him a highly effective servant of the Lord at a time when the Jews desperately needed a hero.

A Life Lesson from Nehemiah

Contagious Christianity

From the day that Nehemiah understood his role in God's plan for the people in Jerusalem, his trust in God's provision and protection was unshakable. His confidence in God was contagious, and the people responded to his faith in God and did their part to rebuild the wall. The completion of the wall was a group effort!

How visible and fervent is your faith? People are looking for "the real thing." Ask God, as Nehemiah did, to give you the courage and strength to live out your faith and inspire others to join with you in your faith and service to Christ.

New Testament

The New Testament is a collection of 27 books that teach the story and significance of God's victory over sin and death through Jesus Christ, the Savior of mankind. The New Testament books were written primarily by some of the apostles or Jesus' half-brothers, and they complete the story the Old Testament began. The Old Testament describes the fall of mankind and God's choice of Israel to represent Him to the nations, and prophesies the coming of Messiah. The New Testament reveals that Messiah—who was also the Son of God, the Savior, the Lord Jesus Christ—came to redeem not just Israel but all the nations through His death and resurrection.

Nile River

The Nile River is made up of two rivers—the Blue Nile and the White Nile—which combine to form the longest river in the world. The White Nile starts at 3720 feet elevation at Lake Victoria in present-day

Uganda, and the Blue Nile comes from Lake Tana in Ethiopia. The two rivers meet near the Sudanese capital, Khartoum, and the Nile flows downhill until it reaches the Mediterranean Sea at sea level after a 4184-mile journey. With its deposits of fertile soil, the Nile has long been an important agricultural resource for Egypt. Because of its life-giving properties, the ancient Egyptians worshiped Hapi, the god of the Nile. When the God of the Bible turned the Nile to blood during the first of the ten plagues, He showed His power over this important but false Egyptian deity. (See Exodus 7:20-21.)

Nineveh

Nineveh, the capital city of the Assyrian Empire, was built by Nimrod, a descendant of Noah. At one point God was going to destroy this vast city, which took three days to walk around and had a population of over 600,000 people. God sent the prophet Jonah to warn the people of their impending doom and their need to repent of their sins. (See *Jonah*.) When the people repented, God had compassion and spared them. But evidently Nineveh's repentance did not last. About 150 years later, in 612 B.C., God let the city be destroyed by the Babylonians and Medes. (See Genesis 10:11; Jonah 3:3; 4:11.)[14]

Noah

Noah lived at a time of terrible wickedness on the earth. God observed that Noah alone was righteous, and He graciously spared Noah and his family from His plan to flood the earth. God told Noah to build an ark (see *Flood*) for protection from the coming destruction. Noah did as God commanded, and according to God's instructions, put animals in the ark (two by two, male and female). The flood came and destroyed all living creatures on the earth. After the flood receded and the ark rested upon the mountains of Ararat, Noah and his family were allowed to leave the ark. God placed a rainbow in the sky as a sign of His promise never to destroy the earth again with a flood. Noah ultimately lived to the age of 950 years before he died. (For Noah's story, see Genesis 5:28–10:32.)

A Life Lesson from Noah

Character Counts!

Noah's righteous character stood out to God in stark contrast to the horrible wickedness of everyone else on the earth. God decided to spare Noah and his family from judgment because of this, demonstrating His compassion for those who are faithful to Him.

O

Occupations of the Bible

We often think of the era of the Bible as a simpler time, and to a degree, that's true. But society still functioned with established trades, and people still had to earn their living. Below are some examples of occupations mentioned in the Bible.

Armorbearer. An armorbearer's job was similar to that of a golf caddy. Just as a caddy carries the clubs of a golfer, an armorbearer carried the weapons of his commanders, and he also killed enemies the commanders had wounded.

Cupbearer. A cupbearer tested all beverages before serving them to the king. Nehemiah was a cupbearer to King Artaxerxes. The job was dangerous because if the drink was poisoned, the cupbearer could die. Therefore a cupbearer was considered to be one of the most important and trusted men in the king's court. (See Nehemiah 1:11.)

Fisherman. Several of Jesus' disciples were professional fishermen. Their occupation was a respected one and met people's need for food. Fishing demanded hard work, was sometimes unfruitful, and required the fishermen to live near water.

Midwife. A midwife helped other women give birth to their children.

Tax collector. Tax collectors were usually hired by a conquering country—in Jesus' day, this was Rome. Their job was to collect taxes for the ruling government. Generally tax collectors were told what to collect for the government, and were allowed to keep for themselves any additional monies they collected. Because their tax rates were usually exorbitant, tax collectors were despised, shunned by the nationals, and ostracized from society. Levi, who became Matthew, was a tax collector who left his post to follow Jesus and become His disciple.

Tent-maker. Tent-making was an ancient trade, and tents were usually made out of a cloth comprised of goat's hair. Paul, Aquila, and Priscilla were New Testament tent-makers. (See Acts 18:2-3.)

Offerings

In the Bible, an offering is a gift or sacrifice dedicated to God. In the book of Leviticus, God describes different kinds of offerings.

Burnt offering. A burnt offering required the use of a sheep, ram, or goat that was perfect and spotless, which could serve as an atonement or any number of other things (See Leviticus 1:1-17.)

Grain offering. A grain offering usually involved no bloodshed, and it was not to be made with leaven. (See Leviticus 2:11.)

Peace offering. A peace offering was given out of thanksgiving for something God had done.

Sin offering. A sin offering was for the atonement for sins. Detailed instructions specified who and how this offering was administered. An anointed priest was to officiate, especially if the sin affected the entire community. Sin offerings were interchangeable with guilt offerings. (See Leviticus 4:3.)

Guilt offering. A guilt offering, also called the trespass offering, was often linked directly with a sin offering. The main difference between the two was that a sin offering dealt with an offense against God that also threatened the community, whereas a guilt offering was more for one individual's violation against God's laws or standards.

One Final Offering

The Ultimate Offering

The blood of bulls and goats was never able to take away the sins of the people. The Old Testament offerings were but a shadow or preview of the ultimate offering that was to come. The Suffering Servant of Isaiah 53:10 was predicted as reconciling man to God. John the Baptist was sent as a herald to this coming Messiah. John pointed to Jesus and called out, "Behold! The Lamb of God who takes away the sin of the world!" (John 1:29). Through Jesus' one offering of Himself, He perfected for all time those who believe in Him. Have you accepted His offer of salvation? He was the ultimate offering, and He offers you the ultimate gift—eternal life!

Old Testament

The Old Testament is a collection of 39 books written mostly in the Hebrew language, with a few verses also written in Aramaic. The Old Testament contains beliefs and teachings (theology) from which the New Testament writers drew. The Old Testament has three parts:

The Historical Books—The first 17 books of the Bible trace the history of man from creation to the inception and destruction of the nation of Israel. In the Pentateuch (the first five books of the Bible), Israel is chosen, redeemed, and prepared to enter a promised homeland. The remaining 12 historical books record the conquest of that land, a transition period during which judges ruled over the nation, the formation of the kingdom, and the division of that kingdom into northern (Israel) and southern (Judah) kingdoms, and finally the destruction and captivity of both kingdoms.

The Poetic Books—The next set of books are not related to historical experiences, but rather to experiences of the human heart. They do not advance the story of the nation of Israel. Instead, through the use of Hebrew poetry, they delve into the questions of suffering, wisdom, life, love, and most importantly, the character and nature of God. Finally, they serve as a hinge linking the history of the past with the prophetic books of the future.

The Prophetic Books—The last division, the Prophets, consists of 17 books and comprises about one-fourth of the Old Testament. The office of prophet was instituted during the days of the prophet Samuel. The prophets stood with the priest as God's special representatives. The men who wrote these books were called or appointed to "speak for" God Himself. God communicated His message to them through a variety of means, including dreams, visions, angels, nature, miracles, and an audible voice. Their messages were meant to expose sin, call the people back to the law of God, warn of coming judgment, and predict the coming of the Messiah. Unfortunately, because of the nature of their messages, the prophets were often violently scorned and their lives endangered.

The Three Parts of the Old Testament

The Historical Books	Theme
Genesis	Beginnings
Exodus	Deliverance
Leviticus	Instruction
Numbers	Journeys
Deuteronomy	Obedience
Joshua	Conquest
Judges	Deterioration and deliverance

Ruth	Redemption
1 Samuel	Transition
2 Samuel	Unification
1 Kings	Disruption
2 Kings	Dispersion
1 Chronicles	Israel's spiritual history
2 Chronicles	Israel's spiritual heritage
Ezra	Restoration
Nehemiah	Reconstruction
Esther	Preservation

The Poetic Books

Job	Blessings through suffering
Psalms	Praise
Proverbs	Practical wisdom
Ecclesiastes	All is vanity apart from God
Song of Solomon	Love and marriage

The Prophetic Books

Isaiah	Salvation
Jeremiah	Judgment
Lamentations	Lament
Ezekiel	The glory of the Lord
Daniel	The sovereignty of God
Hosea	Unfaithfulness
Joel	The day of the Lord
Amos	Judgment

Obadiah	Righteous judgment
Jonah	God's grace to all people
Micah	Divine judgment
Nahum	Consolation
Habakkuk	Trusting a sovereign God
Zephaniah	The "great day of the LORD"
Haggai	Rebuilding the temple
Zechariah	God's deliverance
Malachi	Formalism rebuked

P

Parables

Jesus often taught using plain teaching or sermons, but He also loved to communicate truth through parables. Parables are stories that may or may not be historical, and ultimately serve to make a point. The elements in Jesus' parables were drawn from everyday events or activities that often became symbolic of other things. Most people think of Jesus when they think of parables, but He wasn't the first one to speak in parables. When the prophet Nathan confronted King David about his adultery with Bathsheba, he spoke a pointed parable about a rich man who stole a poor man's sheep. (See 2 Samuel 12:1-4.)

Some of Jesus' better known parables include the parable of the sower, the parable of the wheat and the tares, the parable of the ten minas, the parable of the prodigal son, and the parable of the good Samaritan.[15]

Passover

Passover celebrates God's deliverance of His people from their bondage in the land of Egypt. Before God sent the tenth and final plague upon Egypt—which was the death of the first-born male of every household—the people of Israel were instructed to sacrifice an unblemished or perfect male lamb and sprinkle its blood on their doorposts so that the angel of death would "pass over" their homes and families and not kill the firstborn in the house. Passover is still celebrated by Jews around the world today, and it occurs the first day of the Feast of Unleavened Bread. (See Exodus 12–13. See also *Festivals of the Bible*.)

Paul/Saul

Next to the Lord Jesus Christ, Paul (also known as Saul; see Acts 13:9) of Tarsus, a Jewish Roman citizen, was the most significant figure of the Christian era. He was born about the same time as Jesus, in Tarsus in Asia Minor. Paul was a Pharisee and educated under the rabbi Gamaliel. Initially a persecutor of Christians, Paul became a firm follower of Jesus and one of the greatest missionaries to the Gentiles of his time. Paul first appears in the Bible at the stoning of Stephen, who was an outstanding and outspoken deacon appointed by the apostles of the early church. Paul believed Christians were a threat to Judaism and was supportive of Stephen's death. While on the road to Damascus to arrest Christians, the risen Jesus appeared to Paul and commissioned him to take the message of the Messiah to the Gentiles. Paul was beheaded for his beliefs in Rome around the age of 67. (See Acts 13:9; 7:58; 8:1-3; 9:1-19.)

Paul's missionary journeys. Paul was an extraordinary missionary, taking faithful Christians like Barnabas, John Mark, and Silas along with him as companions and helpers on his journeys. He started many churches along the way, preaching the gospel of Jesus in Jerusalem, Antioch, Athens, Ephesus, Thessalonica, Corinth, and elsewhere. The book of Acts ends with Paul under house arrest in Rome, welcoming all who visited him and telling them the good news of Jesus. (See Acts 28:11-31.)

Paul's epistles. Paul wrote a large portion of the New Testament, including most of the epistles. His letters can be divided into two categories: letters to the churches, and letters to individuals. The language of "justification" and "saved by grace," used in Christian theology, comes from Paul's letters.[16]

A Life Lesson from Paul

Uniquely Prepared to Serve

Paul had an incredible impact on his world—an impact that has continued to this day through his writings. Paul's unique life and abilities were a valuable asset to God, and he held nothing back from God. All of his training, education, intelligence, and personality was used by God. God had a willing servant who gave his all until his last breath.

Like Paul, you have a unique set of gifts and abilities that make you of great value for God's service. Are you willing to let God take your unique life with all its qualities—and shortcomings—and use it for His service? Or are there some areas of your life that you're holding back for yourself? You'll never know all that God can do through you until you allow Him to have every part of you.

Paul's First Missionary Journey
Starting at Selucia, Paul and Barnabas journeyed to various cities, then after reaching Derbe, they went back the same way to Perga, Attalia, then back to Selucia.

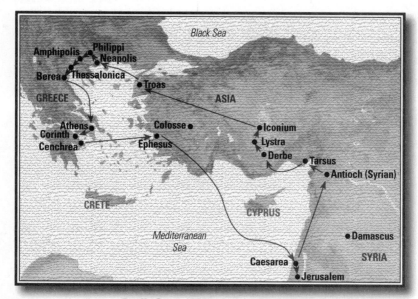

Paul's Second Missionary Journey

Paul and Silas covered much of Asia Minor and went to Greece. At Traos, Paul, Silas, Timothy, and Luke took a ship to Samothrace. Timothy and Silas stayed in Berea, while Paul went on to Athens.

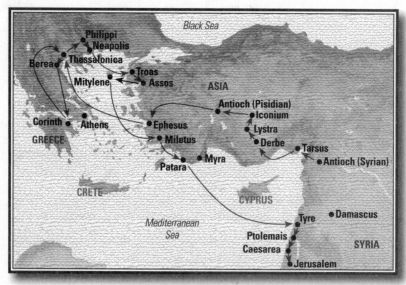

Paul's Third Missionary Journey

Paul visited several churches from previous trips, and ended his journey in Jerusalem.

Persia

Persia is important in biblical history because of its contact with God's people, the Jews. The Jews had been exiled for 70 years to Babylon because of their stubborn rebellion against God. When the time of their exile was over, Cyrus, the king of Persia, became God's instrument in the Jews' release to return to their homeland. Persia conquered Babylon in 539 B.C., and within one year Cyrus decreed that the Jews could return home. The Persian Empire lasted from 550 B.C. to 330 B.C., when it was overthrown by Alexander the Great. (See Ezra 1:1-4.)

Peter/Simon

Simon (later named Peter by Jesus) was a fisherman and native of Bethsaida in the region of Galilee. He and his brother, Andrew, were early disciples of John the Baptist. Simon was introduced to Jesus by Andrew. In predictable fashion, Jesus changed Simon's name to *Cephas*, which in the local dialect of the day meant "rock," and in the Greek translates to "Peter" (Luke 6:14). Peter and Andrew were called by Jesus to become part of the 12 disciples.

Not until after Peter's denial of his affiliation with Jesus (shortly before Jesus' crucifixion) and his restoration by Jesus did Peter's erratic and fiery disposition begin to be redirected as a "rock" to the rest of the disciples. After Jesus' ascension into heaven, Peter became a bold spiritual leader in the church. He regrouped the disciples and preached the resurrection of Jesus on the day of Pentecost, proclaiming to his listeners their need to repent. Peter was unbending in his commitment to spreading the gospel throughout Jerusalem, even in the face of persecution from his fellow Jews. (See Acts 2.)

In Acts chapter 10, we read that God showed Peter through a dream that Gentiles were not unclean (as many Jews of the time thought), and that Gentiles too could come to know Jesus as their Savior. Later, when this issue became a problem, Peter sided with Paul and Barnabas, saying that Gentiles were saved by grace, just as he and his fellow Jews were. Peter wrote two of the letters of the New Testament—1 and 2 Peter. In 1 Peter, he encouraged Christians who were suffering, saying that it was good to be persecuted for Jesus' sake and that they should endure such things. In 2 Peter, he said he and his fellow disciples had not made up the story about Jesus but were eyewitnesses of His majesty. He also exhorted believers to live wisely, to beware of false teachers, and to anticipate the coming day of the Lord. Tradition states that Peter was crucified in Rome. (See John 1:40-42; Acts 15:6-11.)

A Life Lesson from Peter

The God of Second Chances

Peter was characterized as a quick-to-speak, slow-to-listen disciple whose faith crumbled under pressure. But because of Jesus, he was dramatically changed and became a powerful leader in the early church and one of the greatest New Testament leaders.

Aren't you glad God doesn't give up on you when you fail? Peter had great potential, but he often said or did the wrong thing. Yet the God of second chances met him after he had denied Jesus three times, and put him back on the road of service. Are you thinking that you've failed God one too many times and that He won't want to give you another chance? Well, think again! God knows your heart. And He wants to forgive you and see you back in His service. Go to Him now and receive His infinite love and limitless forgiveness. Your service is needed!

Pharisees

The Pharisees were one of the more prominent Jewish sects during

New Testament times. Their defining characteristics included their firm commitment to the Old Testament Scriptures as well as the oral law, which was an attempt to explain the written law. Often they took issue with Jesus for His actions that violated their oral traditions, such as healing people and picking grain on the Sabbath, both of which they considered to be "work" that was forbidden on the Sabbath, according to the law. Jesus criticized the hypocrisy, self-righteousness, and legalistic teaching of many of the Pharisees of His day. The apostle Paul was a Pharisee before he became a Christian, and there were some Pharisees, such as Nicodemus and the rabbi Gamaliel, whom the Bible speaks of positively. Sadly, the Pharisees were involved in the plot to kill Jesus. (See Matthew 12:1-14; John 3:1-7; Acts 5:34-39.)

A Life Lesson from the Pharisees

Being the Real Thing

Many of the Pharisees opposed Jesus because He said that their outward religious show often didn't match their inward character. Jesus called them hypocrites. A hypocrite is one who is two-faced, who appears to be one person while secretly being someone else. Jesus knew the hearts of the Pharisees and exposed them for who they really were.

No one can fool God. He knew the hearts of the Pharisees, and He knows your heart too. What does God see when He looks inside you? Make it a point to be the real thing. If you find yourself being a hypocrite, do something about it. Ask God to give you a pure heart. Then your actions, especially your religious activities, will truly confirm the purity of your heart.

Philippi

The city of Philippi (located in what is now Greece) received its name from Philip II of Macedon (the father of Alexander the Great).

Attracted by the nearby gold mines, Philip conquered the region in the fourth century B.C. In the second century B.C., Philippi became part of the Roman province of Macedonia. The city remained obscure until the famous battle of Philippi (in which the forces of Antony and Octavian defeated those of Brutus and Cassius). After the battle, Philippi became a Roman colony with all the rights and privileges granted to cities in Italy, including citizenship and exemption from taxes.

Philippi was the first European city visited by the apostle Paul on his second missionary journey (see *Paul*), and the church he established there was also the first church he founded in Europe. Later Paul wrote a letter to the Christians in Philippi while he was in prison in Rome, thanking them for their support of his ministry and encouraging them to live a joyous life in Christ. He also described the Christians in Philippi as citizens of heaven, which had great significance because the Philippians prided themselves on being citizens of Rome. (See Philippians 3:20.)

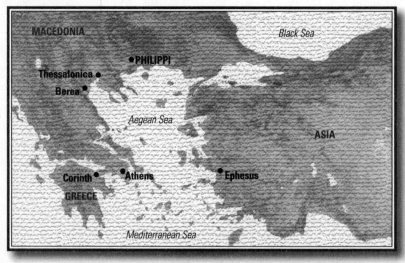

Philippi

Philistines

It is generally believed that the Philistines, mercenaries of mixed ethnic backgrounds who lived throughout the Mediterranean region, migrated from the Aegean Islands to the land of Canaan. There they became neighbors to Israel and frequently fought the people of Israel. One famous example is the battle in which the Philistine giant named Goliath challenged any of King Saul's men to fight him (1 Samuel 17).

Plants of the Bible

Trees of the Garden of Eden. When God created the Garden of Eden, He placed the tree of life and the tree of the knowledge of good and evil in the garden. The tree of life could make man live forever, and it is mentioned later in the book of Revelation in connection with eternal life. God did not forbid Adam and Eve to eat of the tree of life, but He did forbid eating from the tree of the knowledge of good and evil. Sadly, Eve succumbed to the serpent's temptation and ate from the tree of the knowledge of good and evil. Adam also ate from it, causing their expulsion from the garden and sin's entrance into the world. (See Genesis 2:9; 3:22; Revelation 2:7; 22:2.)

Fig tree. The fig tree is still common in Israel today. Jesus once cursed a fig tree for not bearing fruit as it should have, thus making a point to His disciples. (See *Foods of the Bible.*) (See Mark 11:12-14,20-25.)

Olive tree. The olive tree was and is very important in ancient Israel for economic reasons. It grows very slowly, requiring much patience. Paul used the olive tree to compare the Gentiles who had come to faith as branches that had been cut off from a "wild" olive tree and were now grafted into a "cultivated" olive tree (which represented Israel). (See Romans 11:24.)

Sycamore tree. Sycamore trees are susceptible to frost and cold temperatures, so they grow mostly in the lowlands. Zacchaeus, who was short, climbed a sycamore tree so that he could see Jesus in the midst of a crowd (See *Zacchaeus.*) (See Luke 19:4.)

Mustard seed. Jesus referred to the mustard seed as the least of all the seeds. He said that the mustard seed grows into a great tree, making His point that the kingdom of God would start out small, but it would grow immensely, which is exactly what has happened. (See Matthew 13:32.)

Vine. The vine and its fruit have provided wine for liquid sustenance to those in the barren desert country of Israel. The Bible names Noah as a farmer of the vine. The vine was Judea's emblem on coins during the second century B.C. Jesus called Himself the vine, His Father the vinedresser, and those who believe in Him the branches, who are to abide in Him. (See Genesis 9:20; John 15:1-8.)

For more on plants of the Bible, see also *Foods of the Bible.*

Polygamy

Polygamy was common in the ancient world, which influenced the Israelites. Jacob and his marriage to both Rachel and Leah is a classic example. Jacob's brother, Esau, also had more than one wife.

After the patriarchal period (the time of Abraham, Isaac, and Jacob), men still took many wives. But Moses told the people of Israel that their kings should not have numerous wives because they might turn the kings' hearts away from God. When David was king over Israel, he had multiple wives. His son Solomon also had multiple wives—700 of them!—and sadly, they turned his heart away from God. (See Deuteronomy 17:17.)

A Life Lesson from Polygamy

Till Death Us Do Part

The examples of the patriarchs and kings David and Solomon show how problematic polygamy can be. The Bible is filled with instances of wives who didn't get along and children who hated one another. Jesus' model for marriage between one man and one woman comes from Genesis 2:24, which He quoted in Matthew 19:5: "A man shall leave his father and mother and be joined to his wife, and the two shall become one flesh."

Priests

A priest, in the biblical sense, was one who offered sacrifices to God. Under the Levitical priesthood, only Aaron's descendants could be priests. Also, only the high priest could enter the Holy of Holies in the tabernacle and later, the temple. He would do this only once a year to offer sacrifices for all the people of Israel on Yom Kippur, the Day of Atonement. The animal sacrifices offered by the priests had no real effect on people's sins. Not until the Great High Priest—Jesus Christ—came could sin be dealt with once and for all. (See Hebrews 7:26-27.)

Prophecy

A prophecy was a declaration from God concerning either His will for mankind or a future event that would transpire. Jeremiah, for instance, prophetically warned God's people to repent lest they be taken into captivity in Babylon. His declaration announced both God's will and a future event. Isaiah made prophetic declarations about a child who would one day be born of a virgin and suffer and die on behalf of the transgressions of His people. Jesus Christ was that person. Isaiah's prophecy was solely about a future event. There are many other prophecies in the Bible that have yet to be fulfilled. (Isaiah 7:14; 9:6; 52:13–53:12.) (See *Revelation*.)

Prophets

Prophets were chosen by God to serve as His spokesmen. There were two kinds of prophets: those who warned the people against social injustice and failing to follow God or encouraged them to trust God, and those who made predictions. A true prophet was right 100 percent of the time. (See *Prophecy*.)

Proverbs

The book of Proverbs, written mostly by David's son Solomon, contains short sayings or concise observations about life, often contrasting the fool with the wise.

Q

Queen of Sheba

This unnamed queen was so curious about the greatness of King Solomon that she traveled hundreds of miles to meet him, see his vast wealth, and ask him questions. After her encounter with Solomon, she was greatly impressed and glorified his God for what she had seen and heard. (See 1 Kings 10:1-10,13; 2 Chronicles 9:1-9,12.)

Quirinius

Quirinius was the governor of Syria during the time of Jesus' birth. (See Luke 2:2.)

R

Red Sea

The Red Sea (or Sea of Reeds) is a large body of water between the Arabian peninsula and Egypt. During the Exodus, when the Israelites left Egypt, God caused the waters of the Red Sea to part, allowing Moses and the people of Israel to walk through on dry land. He then made the waters crash down on the Egyptian soldiers who were chasing the Israelites, killing them all. (See *Exodus*.) (See Exodus 14:13-31.)

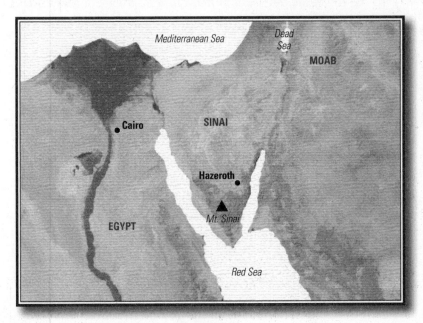

The Red Sea

Repentance

In both Old and New Testaments, the term *repent* means "go the opposite direction." So to repent of one's sins is to turn around and turn to God. When Jesus began His ministry, He preached that all should repent because the kingdom of heaven was at hand. God's grace saves us when we recognize our sin, repent, and turn to Jesus, by whose death we are reconciled to God when we put our faith in Him. (See Matthew 4:17.)

Resurrection

In the Bible, the term *resurrection* can refer to one of two things: Jesus' resurrection, or the general resurrection of the dead at the end of time.

The resurrection of Jesus. Jesus told His disciples that He would suffer, die, and rise from the dead on the third day. All that Jesus said happened just as He predicted. On the morning of the third day, a group of women were the first to come to the empty tomb, followed by Peter and John. Jesus first appeared to Mary Magdalene, then two of the disciples on the road to Emmaus, the rest of the disciples, His half-brother James, and many others. After Jesus ascended into heaven, He also appeared to Paul. All of the early disciples recognized the importance of the resurrection, realizing (as Paul wrote) that if there was no resurrection, all were still dead in their sins. (See Mark 8:31-32; 1 Corinthians 15:3-8.)

The general resurrection of the dead. The prophet Daniel predicted that all mankind would be resurrected, some to everlasting life and the remainder to everlasting judgment. Jesus spoke of this moment many times during His ministry, as did Paul, and John also wrote extensively on it in the book of Revelation. (See Daniel 12:2; John 5:28-29; Acts 24:15.)

Revelation

Revelation is the last book in the Bible and is the grand finale of God's message to man. The title comes from the Greek word meaning "uncovering," "unveiling," or "disclosure." Unlike most books of the Bible, Revelation reveals its own theme in the first verse—"the Revelation of Jesus Christ." The Bible is a literary work and should be read and understood literally like any other piece of written literature, and this includes the prophetic passages and books of the Bible. Revelation 1:19 gives a basic outline of the book's divisions; Jesus instructed the apostle John to write:

- *"the things which you have seen"*—John was to write down what he was seeing in his vision of Jesus (chapter 1);

- *"the things which are"*—John was to write about the seven churches and their present spiritual condition (chapters 2–3);

- *"the things which will take place after this"*—John was to write about the events that would take place at some time in the future (chapters 4–22).

A Life Lesson from Revelation

Last Word, God's Word

Christ's final truth and promise in the book of Revelation, and in the Bible, is presented in Revelation 22:20: "Surely I am coming quickly." What should your response be? The same verse tells you. You, along with the apostle John, should respond, "Amen. Even so, come, Lord Jesus!"

Jesus' Comments to the Seven Churches

(Revelation 2–3)

Church #1: The loveless church—Ephesus
"You have lost your first love" (see 2:4)

Church #2: The persecuted church—Smyrna
"I know how much you have suffered" (2:9)

Church #3: The lax church—Pergamos
"You tolerate sin" (2:14-15)

Church #4: The compromising church—Thyatira
"You permit the teaching of immoral practices" (2:20)

Church #5: The lifeless church—Sardis
"You are dead" (3:1)

Church #6: The obedient church—Philadelphia
"You have...kept My word, and have not denied My name" (3:8)

Church #7: The lukewarm church—Laodicea
"You are neither cold nor hot" (3:15)

The Seven Churches in Revelation 2–3

Roman Empire

The Roman Empire operated under a succession of emperors, beginning with Augustus in 31 B.C. The most famous or well-known leader of Rome was Julius Caesar, whose power was great and conquests were numerous. Because of his strength and power, Julius Caesar paved the way for the shift from a democracy to a dictatorship. His great-nephew, Augustus, became the first emperor of the Roman Empire.

Rome

The city of Rome is located in what is now Italy. Rome was founded in 753 B.C., and by the second century B.C., its leaders had conquered the known world (see *Roman Empire*). The apostles Peter and Paul were both imprisoned and executed in Rome for their faith in Christ.

S

Sabbath

The Bible states that God rested on the seventh day after the creation of the world. In the Ten Commandments, God decreed that all Israel should rest on the seventh day, Saturday, setting it apart as holy. It was known as the Sabbath or *Shabbat* (meaning "cessation"), and no work was to be done during that day. The penalty for working on the Sabbath was death. For instance, a man was put to death for gathering wood on the Sabbath. (See Genesis 2:3; Exodus 20:8; 31:14; Numbers 15:32-36.)

Some people, however, began to treat the Sabbath as a merit badge, ignoring God's other commands while priding themselves on keeping the law of the Sabbath. God expressed anger at this hypocritical observance. Jesus also rebuked the Pharisees for hypocritically condemning His disciples for picking and eating heads of grain on the Sabbath. Jesus followed the true nature of the Sabbath and did not turn it into an exhaustive list of regulations as the Pharisees did. Because Jesus rose from the dead on a Sunday, Christians began to meet on the first day of the week as a special day to worship the Lord. The Jewish community continues to observe Saturday as their Sabbath day. (See Isaiah 1:13; Matthew 12:2-8; Matthew 28:1; Acts 20:7.)

A Life Lesson from the Sabbath

Free to Worship!

Because of Jesus' victory over death on the cross and His resurrection, the death penalty for working on the Sabbath no longer applies.

The important thing for Christians to keep in mind is that the original purpose of the Sabbath was to free people from all distractions so they could focus entirely on God. We are free today to worship God at all times and in all places. It's a matter of the heart—a heart that continually acknowledges God and worships Him. However, we are still to gather regularly with other believers for instruction, encouragement, and fellowship. (See Hebrews 10:25.)

> "Let us not give up meeting together,
> as some are in the habit of doing,
> but let us encourage one another—and all the more
> as you see the Day approaching"
>
> (HEBREWS 10:25).

Sacrifice(s)

See *Offerings*.

Sadducees

The Sadducees were a Jewish sect that existed during the time of Jesus. Unlike the Pharisees (see *Pharisees*), they did not believe in a future resurrection of the dead. The Sadducees accepted only the first five books of the Bible as authoritative, rejecting the Pharisaic notion of an oral law. The Sadducees were in charge of the temple and tried to maintain, for their own interests, a good relationship with the governing Romans.

Salvation

The Bible is a narrative of the saving work of God. In the early pages of Genesis, the first book of the Bible, a prediction was made about how God would send a Savior to redeem fallen man and restore the broken relationship between Himself and man. The rest of the Old Testament is a story of God's choosing to redeem a people from which a Redeemer would appear. The New Testament opens with the birth of the Savior of mankind, Jesus, whose name means "salvation." The New Testament goes on to make it very clear about God's gracious offer of salvation. It is through Jesus' death on the cross, apart from our good works, that we are saved from an eternity apart from God, and it is only through Jesus that we can have eternal life. God's offer of salvation is an incredible gift because it is undeserved. Paul explained that God, in His grace, loves us so much that He sent His Son to pay the penalty for us, rescuing us from eternal condemnation. (See Ephesians 2:8-10, John 14:6; Acts 4:12; Romans 5:8.)

Samson

Samson (whose name means "sunlight") was one of the most famous judges God appointed to protect Israel from enemy nations. (See *Judges.*) God promised a barren couple, Manoah and his wife, that they would have a son, and that he was to be set apart as a Nazirite all his life. (A Nazirite was not to drink wine or cut his hair.) When Samson grew to manhood, he possessed incredible strength.

Unfortunately, Samson used his abilities mostly for his own selfish purposes. Yet God still used Samson to save Israel from the Philistines. His final act of service was to ask God to restore his strength one last time so he could push down the pillars of a Philistine temple. God responded, and Samson was able to push the pillars with all his might so that the entire temple came crashing down, killing him and

3000 Philistines. Samson served as judge of Israel for 20 years. (For Samson's story, see Judges 13–16.)

A Sketch of Samson's Life

His birth: God appeared to his parents.

His hair: As a Nazirite, he was never to cut his hair.

His strength: His power lay in his uncut hair.

His downfall: He loved Delilah, who revealed the secret of power to his enemies.

His shame: He was forced to grind grain like an animal.

His death: He died in one last heroic act while destroying God's enemies.

A Life Lesson from Samson

Living Far from the Edge

Samson was captive to his own passions and pride. However great his gifts were, his flaws and misuse of his gifts were greater. Samson chose to see how close he could get to the edge of obedience by forming compromising relationships and involving himself in questionable things. Though Samson was the strongest man who ever lived, he never lived up to his potential because of his selfish pursuits.

You too have great potential and access to great power from the Lord. Rather than seeing how close you can live to the edge of obedience by making foolish choices or associating with those who can only bring you down to their level of sinful conduct, see how close you can stay to Jesus. Follow Him wholeheartedly. Purpose to live by His Word.

Sanhedrin

The Great Sanhedrin was the ruling Jewish judicial body in Jerusalem during Bible times and was supposed to be made up of the most godly and wise men in Israel. Unfortunately, for the most part, that was not the case. For example, the Sanhedrin violated the Jewish law many times during their trial of Jesus, including bearing false witness and bribing witnesses to tell lies. They also persecuted the followers of Jesus after His resurrection, forbidding them to preach about Jesus. (See Exodus 20:16; Matthew 26:14-16,60-61; Acts 4:17.)

There were members of the Sanhedrin who were careful about their actions, such as Gamaliel, who urged caution about the decision made concerning the disciples, and Joseph of Arimathea, who buried Jesus in his own tomb. (See Acts 5:34-39; Luke 23:50-53.)

Satan

(See also *Devil.*)

Satan (Hebrew: *satan*) simply means "adversary." From the snake of Genesis 3:1 to inciting King David to count the fighting men of Israel—and onward through today—Satan has been the enemy of both God and man, often referred to in Scripture as "the evil one" or "the devil." He was the adversary who challenged God about Job and the accuser of Joshua the high priest. In the New Testament, Satan is called *diabolos,* usually translated as "the devil." This figure tried to tempt Jesus three times in the wilderness, but Jesus resisted him by responding with Scripture each time. The Bible says that Satan (the devil) is a liar and a murderer, disguising himself as an angel of light, prowling about like a roaring lion. He is also called a "great dragon, the serpent of old."

Contrary to popular belief, Satan is not an equal opponent or "arch nemesis" of God. Scripture indicates that Satan must ask permission from God before tormenting or tempting certain people, which suggests that his power is limited. Jesus provided the model for resisting Satan when He combated Satan's lies with Scripture when He was tempted in the wilderness. Jesus brought victory for believers as He came to destroy the works of the devil and render him powerless. Like Jesus, the Bible exhorts us to resist the devil, and he will flee.[17]

Satan has caused havoc for thousands of years and his malicious activities will continue for a time into the future, but his end is coming. God will confine Satan to a place called "the bottomless pit" for 1000 years before he is finally sent to the lake of fire—the final hell prepared for him and his fallen angels. (See Revelation 20:3; 20:10; Matthew 25:41.)

A Picture of Satan Before His Fall

Satan was created by God.

Satan was an exquisite cherubim.

Satan had an exalted position in heaven.

Satan was violent and prideful.

(See Ezekiel 28:12-19.)

Saul, King

God used prophets to speak to the people of Israel for Him and to lead them. But the time came when the people no longer wanted a prophet to lead them. They wanted a king so they could be like all the surrounding nations. This caused the prophet Samuel to go to God about the people's petition because their request for a human king meant they were rejecting God, their divine King. God allowed the request to be granted but warned the people about the dangers of choosing a human king. The man God chose to be the first king over His people was Saul, the son of Kish, of the tribe of Benjamin. Saul was tall and handsome, but he was not obedient to God. When Saul's disobedience persisted, God chose David, the son of Jesse, to replace him. Saul died by killing himself by falling on his own sword in a battle with the Philistines. (See 1 Samuel 8:5; 9:1-2; 31:1-6.)

Life Lessons from Saul

Doing Things God's Way

Saul's disobedience cost him the throne, and his jealousy of David made him obsessed and murderous. He serves as a sad illustration of the consequences of sin and failure to live up to God's standards. Saul was unwilling to do things God's way. He always had a "better idea" and was full of excuses. God doesn't want creative ideas when it comes to obedience. And He doesn't want excuses or rationalizations. God wants complete obedience. He wants things done His way.

Scribes

A scribe ("one who records") was one who kept written records. For example, in the Old Testament, Jeremiah had a scribe named Baruch, who wrote down God's words as Jeremiah dictated. In the New Testament, the apostle Paul used a scribe named Tertius to write his letter to the Romans.

Jewish scribes knew the Hebrew Scriptures well. It was the scribes, along with the chief priests, who were able to tell Herod where the Messiah was to be born. It was also the scribes, along with the Pharisees, whom Jesus condemned for their hypocrisy in valuing their traditions above God's law. (See Jeremiah 36:4; Romans 16:22; Matthew 2:4; 23:13-29.)

Sheol

The Hebrew term *Sheol,* meaning "pit" or "grave," describes the ancient Israelite conception of a continued existence after death. It is associated with darkness, the grave, and death. Jacob was the first to mention Sheol this way. When thinking his son Joseph was dead, Jacob tore his clothes out of grief and said he would go down to Sheol in mourning for his son. David wrote of Sheol in a famous psalm that was fulfilled in Jesus' resurrection. David also believed that it was possible for one to die and go to Sheol in peace. The Old Testament also refers to wicked people going down to Sheol. (See Genesis 37:35; Psalm 16:10; 1 Kings 2:6.)

Shepherd

The Bible speaks frequently of shepherds. A shepherd watches over his sheep (see *Animals of the Bible*) and prevents them from going astray. David was a shepherd, and he acquired great skills in protecting his sheep from wild beasts. David called God his Shepherd, comparing himself to the sheep God cares for. Jesus referred to Himself as the Good Shepherd who sacrifices Himself for His sheep. (See 1 Samuel 16:11; 17:34-36; Psalm 23; John 10:11.)

Sin

In both the Hebrew and Greek languages, the word *sin* means the same thing—"a miss of the mark." Starting with the disobedience of Adam and Eve in the Garden of Eden, all people have "sinned" or "missed the mark" and come short of God's standard. Sin is human defiance of the laws of God, and because God is a God of justice, He cannot leave sin unpunished. Everyone would be doomed to hell because everyone sins, but God sent His Son Jesus to die in their place, presenting the free gift of salvation to those who trust in Him as Savior and Lord. (See Genesis 3:1-13; Romans 3:23; Romans 6:23.)

Sinai, Mount

Also known as Mount Horeb, Mount Sinai was the location where God first talked with Moses at the burning bush, where Moses took the people of Israel after God freed them from slavery in Egypt, and where God gave Moses the law for His people, including the Ten Commandments. Moses spent a lot of time on Mount Sinai, and God frequently talked with Moses there. In fact, after Moses spoke with God on Mount Sinai, his face shone so bright he had to wear a veil when he came back down the mountain to speak to God's people. (See Exodus 3:1-2; 19:2; 34:29-35.)

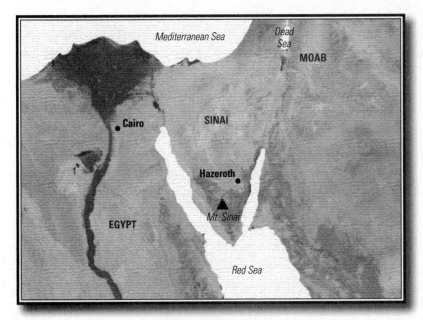

Region of Mt. Sinai

Solomon

Solomon (whose name means "peaceful") was also known as Jedidiah ("beloved of the Lord"). He was one of the sons of King David and became the third king of Israel. He is known as the wisest man who ever lived, apart from Jesus. Before David died, he gave some final instructions to Solomon, encouraging him to walk according to God's commandments.

Solomon began his reign by following his father's wishes. When God offered to give Solomon whatever he wanted, Solomon asked for wisdom. Pleased that Solomon asked for wisdom rather than wealth, God made his wisdom more impressive than anyone else's in the world. He also gave Solomon great wealth, which impressed even the Queen of Sheba, who traveled a long distance to hear his wisdom and see his wealth (see *Queen of Sheba*).

Solomon built the temple in Jerusalem with materials collected by his father David. Unfortunately he didn't continue to take his father's advice and walk in obedience to God. Even though he was wise, he became a fool and made poor choices. He ended up with 700 wives and 300 concubines, and his wives turned his heart away from God, influencing him to serve other gods. This caused God to become angry with Solomon and resulted in God taking away part of Solomon's kingdom and splitting the nation into two—a northern and southern kingdom. But God was still gracious toward Solomon and allowed two tribes, Judah and Benjamin, to remain with the southern kingdom. This was due to God's promise to David, Solomon's father, that one of his descendants would always sit on the throne.

Solomon wrote three of what are referred to as the "wisdom books" of the Bible—Proverbs, Song of Solomon, and Ecclesiastes. He died after a 40-year reign. (See 1 Kings 2:1-9; 2 Chronicles 1:8-13; 1 Kings 4:29-34; 10:1-10; 11:1-13; 12:16.)

━━━━━━━━━━ A Life Lesson from Solomon ━━━━━━━━━━

Bad Company Destroys Good Character

Solomon may have been exceedingly wise, but that didn't make him immune from making poor choices that led to compromising his spiritual beliefs and faithfulness to God. It might have been "politically correct" to forge alliances with the surrounding pagan nations through marriages, but ultimately Solomon's choices of foreign wives turned him away from God.

Choosing the right friends and relationships is very important for growth and maturity in the Christian life. The Bible is correct when it says associations with evil people corrupt good morals. Don't follow Solomon's example by choosing relationships based on expediency or passion. Choose friends who challenge you to greater spiritual growth, who pull you up or encourage you in your Christian life. Ask God to guide you to those people and relationships that will keep you close to Him. (See 1 Corinthians 15:33.)

Synagogue

A synagogue is a place of assembly where Jews gather to worship, pray, and read from the Scriptures. When the temple was destroyed by King Nebuchadnezzar and the Jews were exiled to Babylon, they needed a place to gather together to celebrate Sabbaths and festivals. Most scholars believe that synagogues were developed during this period. Whenever and by whomever they were begun, by Jesus' day, synagogues had been used for worship for a long time. The Gospels indicate that Jesus taught in synagogues. Luke said that the apostle Paul taught in synagogues as well. Synagogues are still used among Jews today as public places of worship. (See Matthew 4:23; Acts 13:14-16; 14:1.)

T

Tabernacle

The tabernacle was the dwelling place that the people of Israel made for God, at His command, while they were in the wilderness during their journey to the Promised Land. It had an outer court with an altar of burnt offerings and a laver, and inside were the Holy Place and the Holy of Holies. In the Holy Place were the lampstand, the table of consecrated bread, and the altar of incense. Separated from the Holy Place by a veil, the Holy of Holies contained the Ark of the Covenant and could be entered only once a year by the high priest. Anyone else who entered would die.

The tabernacle was the place where priestly activities were performed on behalf of the people and where God communed with His people. The tabernacle symbolized God's ultimate decision to come down to earth in the flesh of a man to dwell among men and save them from their sins. (See Exodus 25:8-9; John 1:14.)

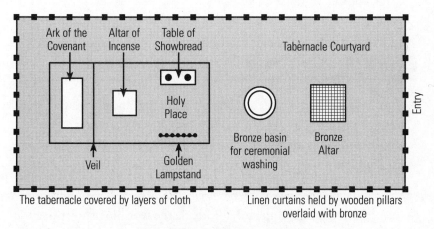

The tabernacle covered by layers of cloth

Linen curtains held by wooden pillars overlaid with bronze

Floor Plan of the Tabernacle

Temple

The first temple was built by King Solomon, and it was patterned after the tabernacle. The tabernacle itself was called "the temple of the Lord." The materials for building the first temple were provided by King David, but his son Solomon built it. The temple was built on Mount Moriah, where God had commanded Abraham to offer up his son Isaac. The first temple was destroyed by Nebuchadnezzar in 586 B.C. when the Jewish people were taken into exile. A new temple was built some 70 years later when many of those taken into exile returned. More than 400 years later, this second temple was significantly refurbished by Herod the Great, a Roman-appointed ruler who wanted to gain the favor of his Jewish subjects. (See Genesis 22:2; 2 Chronicles 2–3; Ezra 6:13-18.)

Jesus used the temple as a metaphor for His own body when He prophesied His death and resurrection. He also prophesied the destruction of the temple by the Romans in A.D. 70. When Jesus died on the cross, the veil in the temple separating the Holy Place from the Holy of Holies was torn from top to bottom, symbolizing that it was now possible for man to become reconciled to God. The Bible also speaks of a future millennial temple (see Ezekiel 40:5–42:20). (See John 2:19-22; Mark 13:1-2; Matthew 27:51.)

Ten Commandments

The Ten Commandments (literally meaning "the ten words") were written with the "finger of God" on two "tablets of stone." The Ten Commandments are listed in Exodus 20:2-17 and Deuteronomy 5:6-21. They are:

1. *"You shall have no other gods before Me."* This was a straightforward commandment that forbade the worship of any other god aside from the one true God. Other "gods" includes

things we think up in our minds, as well as our affection and attention to work, family, money, or anything that holds a higher place in our hearts than God Himself. The theological term for this is *idolatry*, which the apostle John warned his fellow Christians about at the end of his first letter. (See 1 John 5:21.)

2. *"You shall not make for yourself a carved image*—any likeness of anything that is in heaven above, or that is in the earth beneath, or that is in the water under the earth; you shall not bow down to them nor serve them." God's command was not just about idols signifying other gods. He was also talking about images meant to represent Him. The people of Israel violated this commandment when they built a golden calf for themselves and worshiped it. (See Exodus 32.)

3. *"You shall not take the name of the LORD your God in vain,* for the LORD will not hold him guiltless who takes His name in vain." God's name, because it is holy, should never be disrespected or misused in any way. Such disrespect is not limited to using His name as a curse word; it extends to using it in any way that is not honoring to God.

4. *"Remember the Sabbath day, to keep it holy.* Six days you shall labor and do all your work, but the seventh day is the Sabbath of the LORD your God. In it you shall do no work." When God rested from His work of creation on the seventh day, that day became holy. So God wanted everyone to rest on that day as well. By setting aside a day to honor God (today most Christians set aside Sunday because it is the day Jesus rose from the dead), we remember our priority is Him, and not our day-to-day tasks of the work week.

5. *"Honor your father and your mother."* Children are to honor their parents even after they grow up. There is no cutoff point for honoring one's father and mother. No one has perfect

parents, and some people even have bad parents, but regardless of how our parents have treated us, we are not to try and second guess God's command. God says it will go well for us if we obey this command! (See Ephesians 6:1-3.)

6. *"You shall not murder."* All societies have laws against the physical act of murdering other human beings, and for good reason. But Jesus said this commandment was intended not just to condemn the physical act, but to also condemn any unrighteous thoughts of anger we have toward others. (See Matthew 5:21-22; see also Leviticus 19:17-18.)

7. *"You shall not commit adultery."* Jesus said that this commandment also condemns the mere lust after a woman in one's heart. A person commits adultery not just by physically sleeping with someone who is not their spouse, but also by lusting after another person in his or her heart. (See Matthew 5:27-30.)

8. *"You shall not steal."* Stealing is taking something that doesn't belong to you. Stealing can take many different forms, such as taking advantage of someone by getting him to spend a lot of money on you without paying him back, or even something as simple as knowingly taking excessive change from someone. When King David committed adultery with Bathsheba, he also stole her from Uriah, her husband. (See 2 Samuel 11.)

9. *"You shall not bear false witness against your neighbor."* The main thrust of this commandment is against the practice of falsely accusing another person in a court of law, but it also involves speaking a lie against someone else in any context.

10. *"You shall not covet* your neighbor's house; you shall not covet your neighbor's wife...nor anything that is your neighbor's."* Coveting is wanting something that belongs to someone else.

It demonstrates that we aren't happy with what we have, and instead of valuing our neighbor for who he is, or what he has, we think of ways to take it from him.

===== A Life Lesson from the Ten Commandments =====

The Ten Suggestions...or the Ten Commandments?

When God met Moses on Mount Sinai, the first thing He did was give Moses a standard of conduct for him and the people of Israel to follow. The Ten Commandments were not suggestions, but commands that would form the basis for Israel's social and religious structure. As we move into the New Testament era and onward, the question could be asked, "Are the Ten Commandments valid for today?" Jesus answered this question in Mark 12:29-30 when He was asked which of the Ten Commandments was the greatest. Jesus said that, first of all, we are to love God. (This accounts for the first four of the Ten Commandments). He then said we are to love our neighbor. (This accounts for the last six of the Ten Commandments.) Just as God didn't give Moses "the Ten Suggestions," Jesus doesn't give us the right to pick and choose which commands we will or won't obey. The Ten Commandments are important to God, and their observance should be important to you as well!

Ten Plagues

When God sent Moses to Egypt to set the Israelites free from slavery, Pharaoh refused to let the people go. In response, God sent ten plagues upon Egypt, each of which challenged particular Egyptian gods and clearly demonstrated God's power over all the gods of Egypt:

Nile River turned to blood. The Nile River was the source of irrigation water for the fields, so the Egyptians looked upon it as a god, naming it Hapi. God was shown to be more powerful than this false god by turning the Nile to blood. Pharaoh's magicians were able to duplicate this miracle, but no one could drink from the Nile for seven days. (Exodus 7:20-25.)

Frogs. God then unleashed frogs from the Nile upon the land. The Egyptian goddess Heqet was depicted as a frog who assisted with fertility, so in this plague, God proved He has dominion over both fertility and frogs. The Pharaoh's magicians successfully duplicated this plague as well, but they couldn't contain the problem. They only made it worse, just as they did when the Nile was turned to blood. (See Exodus 8:1-15.)

Gnats. Through Aaron, God then turned the dust of the earth into small insects that covered Egypt. These could have been gnats or mosquitoes or some other kind of bug. The god challenged here is probably Thoth, the Egyptian god of magic, because the magicians could not bring forth gnats. (See Exodus 8:16-19.)

Flies. God then unleashed flies upon Egypt. Ptah, who according to Egyptian mythology created the world, apparently could not stop this plague—it's not certain, though, that this is the specific god challenged here. (See Exodus 8:20-32.)

Livestock. God then struck down the livestock of Egypt, which probably challenged the Egyptian gods Hathor and Apis, the former depicted as a cow, and the latter depicted as a bull. (See Exodus 9:1-7.)

Boils. The plague of boils (which could have been skin anthrax) could not be stopped by any of Egypt's deities. Perhaps Imhotep, who was deified after his death and considered the god of healing, was challenged here. (See Exodus 9:8-12.)

Hail. God then sent relentless hail upon the Egyptians, and the goddess of the sky, Nut, could have been the one specifically targeted here. (See Exodus 9:13-35.)

Locusts. God next sent locusts upon Egypt, which devastated the crops. Perhaps this challenged Min, the god of fertility. (See Exodus 10:1-20.)

Three days of darkness. God caused Egypt to endure three days of darkness, an event that showed that Ra, the sun god, was powerless to stop it. (See Exodus 10:21-29.)

Death of the firstborn. This was the final and worst of all the plagues. God warned that if the people of Israel did not put lamb's blood on their doorposts, the angel of death would kill their firstborn. Only if they put blood on their doorposts would the angel of death "pass over" their house (see *Passover*). Not even Pharaoh's firstborn son could escape this plague, even though Pharaoh was considered a god himself. This plague judged all the gods of Egypt (12:12), but it specifically targeted Pharaoh, showing him that God was powerful over everything, including men who think they are gods. This plague finally caused Pharaoh to relent and let God's people go. (See Exodus 11:1–12:32.)

A Life Lesson from the Ten Plagues

God's Offer of Grace

When Moses asked Pharaoh to let the people of Israel go, Pharaoh hardened his heart and said no. So God sent the ten plagues. With each plague, God allowed Pharaoh the opportunity to honor Moses' request that God's people be allowed to leave. Each time, however, Pharaoh hardened his heart in stubborn rebellion. But then we notice something different before the last two plagues: The Bible says *God* hardened Pharaoh's heart (Exodus 10:20). God was no longer extending His grace to Pharaoh and the Egyptians. With the last two plagues, God demonstrated His judgment on both Pharaoh and the Egyptians.

Today, God is still gracious and still desires that unbelievers respond to His offer of life. He still desires that no one should perish. But like God's offer to Pharaoh, His grace will not always be there. Have you accepted His offer of grace through Jesus Christ? Why not do it now?

Thessalonica

Thessalonica was an important city in ancient Macedonia, located on the northwestern side of the Aegean Sea on the main east-west highway leading to Rome. It was originally built by Cassander of Macedon in 315 B.C., who named it after his wife, the daughter of King Philip.

The apostle Paul first visited Thessalonica on his second missionary journey and witnessed to both Jews and Greeks at a synagogue there, reasoning from the Scriptures with them about Jesus being the Messiah. After he established a church at Thessalonica, Paul wrote two letters to the Thessalonians, which make up two books of the Bible, 1 and 2 Thessalonians. (See Acts 17:1-4.)

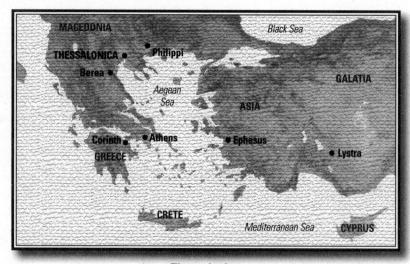

Thessalonica

Timothy

The New Testament speaks of a disciple in Lystra named Timothy (meaning "honored by God"). He was the son of a Jewish woman who was a believer and a father who was a Greek. He was also well spoken of by those in the churches in Lystra and Iconium. (See Acts 16:1-2.)

Paul wanted Timothy to travel with him as a fellow missionary, so he took him along for assistance and ministry. Timothy is mentioned as a traveling companion throughout the rest of the book of Acts. Paul referred to him as a "fellow worker," a "beloved and faithful son in the Lord," one who was "like-minded" to Paul, and "a true son in the faith." Paul wrote several of his letters with Timothy present, and he also wrote two letters directly to Timothy while he pastored the church at Ephesus, instructing him about leaders and behavior in the church. Paul was deeply fond of Timothy, and he valued him immensely as a coworker in spreading the gospel. (See Romans 16:21; 1 Corinthians 4:17; Philippians 2:19-20; 1 Timothy 1:2.)

A Life Lesson from Timothy

What's Really Important?

Paul saw young Timothy as his son in the faith, and he acted as a mentor to Timothy, helping him grow spiritually and encouraging him in what was important in his service to God. Paul's advice to Timothy stands for you today as well as it did to Timothy all those centuries ago: "Let no one look down on your youthfulness, but rather in speech, conduct, love, faith, and purity, show yourself an example of those who believe" (1 Timothy 4:12 NASB).

Travel in Bible Times

Traveling by land. In Bible times, most travel by land was done on foot. Moses led the people of Israel on foot as they traveled through the wilderness, and most soldiers would walk to where they needed to go. Jesus and His disciples regularly walked by foot. To travel by foot, however, was risky, because bandits and robbers were always eager to ambush unsuspecting travelers. Typically a person could walk about 20 miles a day, and it would probably have taken a few days to walk the entire north-to-south length of Israel. Today, one can easily drive the length of Israel in a few hours, depending on the vehicle's speed.

Donkeys were also widely used in Bible times for travel. Probably the most famous example is Balaam and his talking donkey. Mules were also used for travel. Absalom, David's son, was riding a mule when it went under the thick branches of a large tree, causing Absalom to get stuck in the branches. Horses aren't mentioned as a means of transportation until after Israel was split into two kingdoms, which means that they might not have been in common use until that time. The chariot appeared early in the 1000s B.C., and its convenience for travel was marked by its relatively simple design. It had a big wheel on each side of its body and was usually pulled by two horses. The court official of the queen of the Ethiopians was traveling back home in a chariot when Philip shared the gospel of Christ with him. The chariot was commonplace in ancient Middle Eastern battles. (See Numbers 22:22-30; 2 Samuel 18:9; Acts 8:26-39.)

Traveling by sea. Sea travel was not common among the ancient Israelites. We do know, however, that Solomon made use of ships as a means of trade, and the prophet Jonah was able to travel by sea to Tarshish. In the New Testament, Jesus and His disciples (most of whom were fishermen) used boats to get around on the Sea of Galilee, where Jesus performed some of His miracles. Paul and his companions also went on sea voyages to get to some of their destinations, and on one occasion ended up shipwrecked on the island of Malta. The Romans, of course, were expert seafarers, but traveling by sea was never an easy task. (See 1 Kings 10:22; Jonah 1:1-3; Matthew 8:18-27; Acts 27:14–28:10.)

Tribes of Israel, Twelve

The 12 tribes of Israel came from the 12 sons of Jacob, who was renamed *Israel* by God in Genesis 32:24-32. The 12 sons—or tribes—are:

Reuben. Reuben (whose name means "see, a son") was the firstborn of Jacob's 12 sons, whom Jacob had by Leah. Leah gave him this name because God saw that Jacob did not love her as much as Rachel, so He gave her a son. As a boy, Reuben caused tension between Leah and Rachel. And later, when Jacob's eleventh son, Joseph, told his brothers about dreams in which his brothers bowed down to him, some of the brothers concocted a plan to kill him. (See Genesis 29:30-32; 30:14-16; 37:1-11,18.)

However, Reuben, because of his protective nature, prevented the other brothers from carrying out their plan. Instead, he told them to throw Joseph into a pit, secretly planning to rescue him from it later to take him back to their father. His plan backfired, however, when the other brothers decided to sell Joseph into slavery. When Reuben returned and did not see Joseph in the pit, he tore his clothes out of grief.

Years later, when Reuben and his brothers were captured in Egypt while trying to buy food, Reuben reminded his conspiring brothers that he had warned them not to hurt the boy Joseph. He said that their capture was their payment for their sin against Joseph. This was before the brothers realized their captor was Joseph himself!

Before the brothers made the trip to Egypt, Reuben promised his father, Jacob, that he would protect Jacob's youngest son, Benjamin. (See Genesis 37:18-22,25-29; 42:22,37.)

Simeon. Simeon (whose name means "hearing") was the second son of Jacob and Leah. Leah named him Simeon because God "heard" that she was unloved and provided her with another son. He was among the conspiring brothers who had first planned to put Joseph to death but instead sold him into slavery.

Levi. Levi (whose name means "attached") was the third son of Jacob and Leah. Leah named him Levi because she thought this birth would cause her husband to become attached to her. Moses and Aaron and many other prominent people came from Levi's line. The Israelite priesthood also came from the "sons of Levi." (See Exodus 2:1-2; Deuteronomy 21:5).

Judah. Judah (meaning "celebrated") was the fourth son of Jacob and Leah. His mother praised God for his birth. Jacob blessed Judah, indicating that from his tribe would come a king and leader—Jesus Christ—saying,

> Judah, you are he whom your brothers shall praise; your hand shall be on the neck of your enemies...The scepter shall not depart from Judah...until Shiloh comes; and to Him shall be the obedience of the people (Genesis 49:8,10).

Issachar. Issachar (whose name means "he will bring a reward") was the fifth son of Jacob and Leah. Jacob said that he would be "a strong donkey." (See Genesis 49:14.)

Zebulun. Zebulun (whose name means "dwelling") was the sixth son of Jacob and Leah. Jacob predicted that Zebulun would dwell in an area that was beneficial due to seatraders moving through his land. (See Genesis 49:13.)

Dan. Dan (whose name means "judge") was Jacob's first child through Rachel, which she gained through her maid Bilhah. Rachel called him Dan because she felt that God had judged her rightly by giving her a son. Jacob prophesied that Dan would judge his people as one of the tribes of Israel. Samson, a judge, was from the tribe of Dan. (See Genesis 49:16.)

Naphtali. Naphtali (whose name means "my wrestling") was Rachel's second child through her maid Bilhah. She named him Naphtali because of the "wrestling" between her and her sister regarding child-bearing. Jacob prophesied that Naphtali would be a military force marked by speed and power. (See Genesis 49:21.)

Gad. Gad (whose name means "fortune") was the first child born of Leah's maid Zilpah. Jacob, his father, said Gad and his tribe would become valiant fighters worthy of their victories. (See Genesis 49:19.)

Settlement of the Tribes of Israel
The tribe of Levi did not receive an allotment of land, but instead, was given cities to dwell in (see Joshua 14:3-4).

Asher. Asher (whose name means "happy") was the second child born of Leah's maid Zilpah, and Jacob prophesied of him that his tribe would become rich through producing special foods for commerce. (See Genesis 49:20.)

Joseph. Joseph (whose name means "he will add" or "may he add") was the first child naturally born to Rachel. He was Jacob's favorite son out of the 11 sons he had so far. Jacob presented him with a beautiful multicolored coat, which provoked the brothers to jealousy. And when Joseph shared with his brothers about dreams in which they all served him, they became even angrier. They were so upset that they sold him into slavery.

Joseph was sold to Potiphar in Egypt, and became his slave. Even though Joseph served Potiphar well, the unjust actions and accusations of Potiphar's wife led to Joseph being sent to prison. While in prison, Joseph had an opportunity to interpret the Pharaoh's dreams, and as a result he rose to second-in-command of all Egypt. He had predicted a seven-year famine in the land and stored up grain to preserve Egypt from the famine, and sure enough, the famine came.

When Joseph's brothers traveled from Canaan to Egypt to buy grain during the famine, Joseph tricked them by taking advantage of the fact they did not recognize him. Joseph accused them of being spies. But he later revealed his identity, and he forgave his brothers, pointing out that even though they had meant him harm, God had used their evil for good, making it possible for Joseph to become a leader in Egypt and store up grain that would save people—including Jacob's family—from the famine. Before Jacob died, he gave Joseph a very lengthy blessing. (See Genesis 50:20; 49:22-26.)

Benjamin. As Rachel lay dying while giving birth to Benjamin, she called him *Ben-Oni* (meaning "son of my shame") with her last breath. But Jacob, his father, called him *Benjamin*, which means "son of the right hand" or "son of the south."

When Joseph was in disguise and accusing his brothers of being spies, he wanted them to prove they were innocent men by bringing Benjamin to him. Then Joseph revealed himself to his brothers, the charade was over, and the brothers were forgiven for what they had done to Joseph.

Jacob prophesied that Benjamin would be like a wolf who devours prey and divides the spoil. Even though we aren't told much about Benjamin himself, this verse predicted that Benjamin's offspring would be very aggressive. Israel's first king, Saul, was from the tribe of Benjamin, and so was the apostle Paul. (See Genesis 35:18-19; 49:27.)

Tribulation

In the Bible, the term "tribulation" can refer to one of two things:

General tribulation. The Bible often speaks of times of tribulation in the sense of turmoil we experience in general. For example, the apostle Paul wrote that we are to "glory in tribulations" because of the spiritual growth such difficulties produce. Jesus also encouraged the church at Smyrna during its time of "tribulation" or suffering, promising the people there that their tribulation would last only ten days. (See Romans 5:3-4; Revelation 2:9-10.)

The Great Tribulation. Jesus said that one day there will be a great tribulation of a magnitude and intensity that has not been seen since the beginning of the world or ever shall be seen again. This period, known as the Great Tribulation, is described in detail throughout the book of Revelation and will end with Jesus throwing Satan into the lake of fire. (See Matthew 24:21-22; Revelation 7:14; 20:10.)

U

Unleavened Bread

Also known as *matzah,* unleavened bread (bread without yeast, making it flat) is eaten at every Passover by the Jewish people to commemorate their deliverance from slavery in Egypt. God gave Moses specific instructions about the meal the Israelites were to eat on the night that the angel of death would strike the firstborn of Egypt and also of any house that did not have blood smeared on the doorpost. The bread that Jesus and His disciples ate at Passover was most likely unleavened, for they were all Jews. (See Exodus 12; Matthew 26:26.)

Life Lessons from Unleavened Bread

Positive and Negative Influences

Because unleavened bread is bread without leaven or yeast, the bread would be "unaffected" and therefore not rise. In light of this, Jewish teachers would sometimes compare leaven to growth or infestation, depending on whether the sense was positive or negative.

- Jesus warned His disciples to beware of the negative leaven of the Pharisees and their doctrine. On a different occasion, He compared the positive kingdom of heaven to leaven. (See Matthew 16:6-12; 13:33.)

- Paul urged his readers to clean out the old leaven of malice and wickedness and replace it with the positive qualities of sincerity and truth, which he compared to unleavened bread. (See 1 Corinthians 5:6-8.)

▶ Paul also said that "a little leaven leavens the whole lump," pointing out to the Galatians how quickly the false teaching of the Judaizers had spread among them. (See Galatians 5:9.)

V

Vessels

A vessel is a container of some type. Vessels could be made out of varied materials, such as bronze, gold, silver, or, more commonly, wood or clay. Below are some examples of vessels used in Bible times:

Clay jars for scroll or food preservation. The Dead Sea Scrolls, which were discovered around 1946–47 in the caves of Qumran near the Dead Sea, were put in clay jars by a Jewish community at Qumran about a century or more before the time of Jesus. These scrolls contained various texts of the Bible, and even an entire scroll of the book of Isaiah. The clay jars in which the scrolls had been placed were incredible at preserving the scrolls from the destructive elements that would otherwise have destroyed them. Food was also kept safe in clay containers.

Baskets. Baskets carried food and other items. If the basket were big enough, it could carry a human being. As a baby, Moses was placed in a basket of papyrus, which his mother placed in some reeds by the Nile River's bank. Paul escaped from persecutors when his friends lowered him from a window in a large basket. (See Genesis 40:16-17; Exodus 2:3; Acts 9:25.)

Wineskins. Wineskins were made from goat skin and held wine until it fermented. Because the fermentation process stretched the skin, new wine could not be poured into an old wineskin, or the pressure would burst the no-longer-elastic wineskin. Jesus spoke of wineskins to make a point to His hearers that old wineskins were old human traditions and ceremonies that did not appropriately fit in the new wineskins of the New Covenant, which Jesus had come to inaugurate. (See Matthew 9:17.)

Water pitchers. When going to get water, women would often carry water pitchers, which usually had two handles. Jesus once asked a Samaritan woman for a drink of water, which indicates that she was probably carrying a pitcher. (See Genesis 24:14-15; John 4:7.)

Basins. A basin, or bowl, could hold a variety of liquids, usually used for ritual or domestic purposes. There were bronze basins in the tabernacle, and Jesus washed His disciples' feet using a basin filled with water. (See Exodus 27:3; John 13:5.)

Virgin Birth

The Bible reports that Jesus' birth occurred as follows: After His mother Mary was betrothed or engaged to Joseph and before they came together physically in marriage, she was found to be "with child of the Holy Spirit." In other words, Joseph was simply Jesus' adoptive father—the Holy Spirit was responsible for the birth of Jesus. Matthew wrote that this was a fulfillment of biblical prophecy, quoting Isaiah 7:14: "Behold, the virgin shall be with child, and bear a Son, and they shall call His name Immanuel." Several hundred years after Isaiah's prophecy, Jesus was born to a virgin. (See Matthew 1:18,23.)

Importance of the Virgin Birth

The virgin birth is important because Immanuel—"God with us"—is the person of Jesus Christ, who is God in the flesh and literally "God with us." If Jesus had been born of a man and a woman in the natural way, He would have been no more special than the many human prophets in the Old Testament. Only an infinite sacrifice could atone for infinite sin. The virgin birth provided this most special of all people, the God-man, Jesus, as that sacrifice.

W

Warfare in the Bible

Because warfare in Bible times depended on primitive technology, a lot more planning had to take place before battles. Physical conditions such as terrain and rain and cold conditions played a significant role in determining when battles could be fought. For instance, conditions in the desert were harsh, providing numerous challenges, such as those Joshua encountered when he led the people of Israel in battle against the Canaanites. Soldiers made frequent use of armorbearers (see *Occupations of the Bible*), but that made things only a little easier for the fighting men. As king of Israel, David led many conquests, especially with his military commander Joab, who proved to be so bloodthirsty that he and his armorbearers ended up killing David's rebellious son Absalom when he was caught in a tree, provoking David to grief.

Not only did the Israelites battle the surrounding pagan nations throughout their ancient history, they also fought each other in a civil war that took place when the kingdom split in two after Solomon's reign. The Bible informs us that there will be wars and rumors of wars until the end of time, when the Messiah returns. (See Joshua 6; 2 Samuel 18:14-15; Matthew 24:4-8.)

Wrath of God

Paul wrote about the wrath of God in the New Testament, noting that this wrath is revealed from heaven against all ungodliness and unrighteousness. God's wrath is not spiteful vengeance, but holy justice. It is a common misconception among people today that God was wrathful in the Old Testament and loving in the New Testament. The truth is that in both testaments God is both a God of mercy and a God of wrath. For example, in the book of Exodus we learn that God is compassionate and forgives sin, and also that He unleashes His wrath against all the wicked. If it weren't for His Son's debt-canceling death on the cross, all would suffer His wrath eternally because all have sinned and come short of God's standard. But thankfully, those who accept Jesus as Lord and Savior are no longer "children of wrath." They are made alive together with Christ, saved by His grace. (See Romans 1:18; Exodus 34:6-7; Romans 3:23; Ephesians 2:3,5.)

X

Xerxes

Xerxes (also known as Ahasuerus) ruled Persia from 486 to 465 B.C. He is known for his many failed attempts at expanding his empire and his conflicts with Greece, both of which had a negative impact on Persia's economy. The book of Esther relates how Xerxes was displeased with his wife, Vashti, so he replaced her with the Jewess, Esther. Esther used her position with Xerxes to save her people from a wicked plot devised by the evil Haman (see *Esther*).

Y

Yahweh

See *God, Names of.*

Z

Zacchaeus

Zacchaeus was a rich chief tax collector of small stature. One day, when Jesus was passing through Jericho, Zacchaeus tried to see Jesus but couldn't because he was too short to see over the crowds. So he climbed a sycamore tree for a better vantage point. As Jesus passed by the tree, He looked up at Zacchaeus and told him to come down, "for today I must stay at your house."

Zacchaeus was delighted to receive Jesus at his home, but some people complained about Jesus' decision, saying that He was going to the home of a sinner. In those days, it was common for tax collectors to get rich by taking advantage of people, and Zacchaeus was guilty of doing that. Zacchaeus felt convicted and told Jesus he would give half of his goods to the poor and return four times whatever he had taken from anyone falsely. Jesus saw Zacchaeus' sincerity and announced to him that "today salvation has come to this house, because he also is a son of Abraham; for the Son of Man came to seek and to save that which was lost." (See Luke 19:5-10.)

A Life Lesson from Zacchaeus

Why Jesus Came

Jesus apparently had such a profound impact on Zacchaeus that he told Jesus he would dramatically change his ways. Jesus' comment that Zacchaeus "also is a son of Abraham" demonstrated that Jesus was not interested in looking for pious people who paraded their righteousness. Instead, He was looking for the lost, who recognized their sinfulness and wanted to repent and turn to God.

Zacharias

Zacharias was a priest of the division of Abijah. He and his wife Elizabeth (see *Elizabeth*) had no children, and at the time we meet them in the Bible, Elizabeth was old and barren. One day, while Zacharias was performing priestly duties in the temple, the angel Gabriel appeared to him and said that Elizabeth would bear a son named John, who would preach repentance and be the forerunner to the Messiah. Zacharias did not believe Gabriel because he and his wife were too old to have children. Gabriel told Zacharias that as an angel, he stood in the presence of God and had come to bring him this good news from God. Gabriel also said that because Zacharias did not believe the news, he would be unable to speak until the baby was born. Sure enough, from that moment onward Zacharias was not able to speak, and could only make signs to those around him. (See Luke 1:5-23.)

After the son was born to both Zacharias and Elizabeth, their neighbors and friends were thinking he should be named after his father. Elizabeth insisted, however, that his name be John, just as the angel had instructed. But the neighbors and friends argued that no one among her relatives had that name. Finally they asked Zacharias what the child's name should be. Zacharias wrote, "His name is John" on a tablet. Immediately God opened Zacharias' mouth and allowed him to speak again, and he began praising God and prophesying. (See Luke 1:57-79.)

Life Lessons from Zacharias

Faithful No Matter What

Like Abraham and Sarah, Zacharias and Elizabeth were both very old and beyond the normal age for childbearing when they gave birth to a son. But with God, all things are possible. Zacharias had to learn the hard way that unbelief has a price. But when God reopened his mouth, Zacharias responded in praise, knowing that this was a momentous event for Israel. What are some important lessons you can learn from Zacharias?

▸ When you don't get what you want, use your energy and emotions to remain faithful to God in your present situation, as Zacharias and Elizabeth did. They were both righteous before God, walking in all the commandments of the Lord, and blameless in their conduct and attitudes. (See Luke 1:6.)

▸ Believe God when He says something. What you read in the Bible is truth. Don't do as Zacharias did and question God or doubt His message. Put your faith and trust in God's Word, even when you don't understand it.

▸ Your mouth is meant to be used for more than verbal communication with others. It's also to be opened and overflowing with praise. After nine-plus months of being unable to speak, Zacharias' first words affirmed God's choice for his son's name. Then began an outpouring of pure praise.

Zechariah

Zechariah was one of three prophets (the other two being Haggai and Malachi) who communicated their message to the Jews who had returned to Jerusalem from exile in Babylon. Zechariah encouraged the people to finish rebuilding the temple, which had been started by the people when they returned, but then had been left to neglect. He also spoke of the coming Messiah, Jesus, who would rescue His people and reign over all the earth. Zechariah wrote this message in the book that carries his name. The first eight chapters were written around 520–518 B.C., and chapters 9–14 were written around 480 B.C.

Prophecies of Christ's Comings

Christ's First Coming:	Zechariah 3:8
	Zechariah 9:9,16
	Zechariah 11:11-13
Christ's Second Coming:	Zechariah 6:12
	Zechariah 12:10
	Zechariah 13:1,6
	Zechariah 14:1-21

Zion

Zion was the name of the hill in the city of Jerusalem that David captured from the Jebusites. Psalm 2:6 describes Zion as God's holy mountain. The term *Zion* is also sometimes used to refer to the whole nation of Israel. Zion was seen as the home of the Jewish people, and, especially during the exile and throughout the dispersion of the Jewish people, it was seen as synonymous with Jerusalem. The phrase "daughter of Zion" refers to the Jewish captives taken away to Babylon.

When people use the term *Zionist* today, they are referring to someone who believes that the Jewish people have a right to the land of Israel because God had promised Abraham long ago that he would be given that land as an eternal inheritance. (See 2 Samuel 5:7; Psalm 102:13; Isaiah 1:27; Lamentations 4:22; Genesis 15:18-21.)

A Bare Bones Outline of Ancient Israel's History

Note: All dates are approximate, especially those prior to the time of David. Some Bible scholars have suggested different dates for the earliest events below, such as the exodus, depending on how they interpret biblical chronology.

c. 2000 B.C.	God calls Abraham to go to the Promised Land (Canaan)
c. 1440	People of Israel leave Egypt
c. 1400	Joshua leads Israel on conquest of Canaan
13th to 11th centuries B.C.	Time of the judges
c. 1000	David makes Jerusalem his capital, rules 40 years
c. 971-931	Solomon rules for 40 years, builds first temple
c. 931	Israel splits into northern and southern kingdoms
722	Northern ten tribes taken into captivity by Assyria
605, 597, 586	Southern tribes taken into captivity by Babylon in 3 stages
586	Jerusalem and first temple destroyed by Babylon
c. 605-536	70-year captivity in Babylon
516	Second temple is finished by Jews who returned from exile

445	Nehemiah helps rebuild walls of Jerusalem
332	Alexander the Great conquers Jerusalem
170	Antiochus IV, the Seleucid king of Syria, and his soldiers defile the temple
165	Judas Maccabaeus leads a revolt against Seleucids; restores, cleans, rededicates the temple
63	Roman emperor Pompey conquers Jerusalem, Israel under Roman rule
20	Herod the Great begins to expand and lavishly refurbish the second temple, a project that continues for the next 70-80 years
c. 3-0	Jesus is born
c. 30-33 A.D.	Jesus completes His ministry—crucifixion, resurrection, and ascension into heaven
70 A.D.	Roman general Titus destroys second temple
90 A.D.	The apostle John finishes the last of the New Testament

A One-Year
Daily Bible Reading Plan

Genesis

- ❏ 1   1–3
- ❏ 2   4–7
- ❏ 3   8–11
- ❏ 4   12–15
- ❏ 5   16–18
- ❏ 6   19–22
- ❏ 7   23–27
- ❏ 8   28–30
- ❏ 9   31–34
- ❏ 10   35–38
- ❏ 11   39–41
- ❏ 12   42–44
- ❏ 13   45–47
- ❏ 14   48–50

Exodus

- ❏ 15   1–4
- ❏ 16   5–7
- ❏ 17   8–11
- ❏ 18   12–14
- ❏ 19   15–18
- ❏ 20   19–21
- ❏ 21   22–24
- ❏ 22   25–28
- ❏ 23   29–31
- ❏ 24   32–34
- ❏ 25   35–37

❏ 26	38–40

Leviticus

❏ 27	1–3
❏ 28	4–6
❏ 29	7–9
❏ 30	10–13
❏ 31	14–16

February

❏ 1	17–20
❏ 2	21–23
❏ 3	24–27

Numbers

❏ 4	1–2
❏ 5	3–4
❏ 6	5–6
❏ 7	7–8
❏ 8	9–10
❏ 9	11–13
❏ 10	14–15
❏ 11	16–17
❏ 12	18–19
❏ 13	20–21
❏ 14	22–23
❏ 15	24–26
❏ 16	27–29
❏ 17	30–32
❏ 18	33–36

Deuteronomy

❏ 19	1–2
❏ 20	3–4
❏ 21	5–7
❏ 22	8–10
❏ 23	11–13
❏ 24	14–16
❏ 25	17–20

❏ 26   21–23
❏ 27   24–26
❏ 28   27–28

March

❏ 1   29–30
❏ 2   31–32
❏ 3   33–34

Joshua
❏ 4   1–4
❏ 5   5–7
❏ 6   8–10
❏ 7   11–14
❏ 8   15–17
❏ 9   18–21
❏ 10   22–24

Judges
❏ 11   1–3
❏ 12   4–6
❏ 13   7–9
❏ 14   10–12
❏ 15   13–15
❏ 16   16–18
❏ 17   19–21

Ruth
❏ 18   1–4

1 Samuel
❏ 19   1–3
❏ 20   4–6
❏ 21   7–9
❏ 22   10–12
❏ 23   13–14
❏ 24   15–16
❏ 25   17–18
❏ 26   19–20

❑ 27	21–23
❑ 28	24–26
❑ 29	27–29
❑ 30	30–31

2 Samuel

❑ 31	1–3

April

❑ 1	4–6
❑ 2	7–10
❑ 3	11–13
❑ 4	14–15
❑ 5	16–17
❑ 6	18–20
❑ 7	21–22
❑ 8	23–24

1 Kings

❑ 9	1–2
❑ 10	3–5
❑ 11	6–7
❑ 12	8–9
❑ 13	10–12
❑ 14	13–15
❑ 15	16–18
❑ 16	19–20
❑ 17	21–22

2 Kings

❑ 18	1–3
❑ 19	4–6
❑ 20	7–8
❑ 21	9–11
❑ 22	12–14
❑ 23	15–17
❑ 24	18–19
❑ 25	20–22
❑ 26	23–25

1 Chronicles

- ❏ 27   1–2
- ❏ 28   3–5
- ❏ 29   6–7
- ❏ 30   8–10

May

- ❏ 1   11–13
- ❏ 2   14–16
- ❏ 3   17–19
- ❏ 4   20–22
- ❏ 5   23–25
- ❏ 6   26–27
- ❏ 7   28–29

2 Chronicles

- ❏ 8   1–4
- ❏ 9   5–7
- ❏ 10   8–10
- ❏ 11   11–14
- ❏ 12   15–18
- ❏ 13   19–21
- ❏ 14   22–25
- ❏ 15   26–28
- ❏ 16   29–31
- ❏ 17   32–33
- ❏ 18   34–36

Ezra

- ❏ 19   1–4
- ❏ 20   5–7
- ❏ 21   8–10

Nehemiah

- ❏ 22   1–3
- ❏ 23   4–7
- ❏ 24   8–10
- ❏ 25   11–13

Esther

- ❏ 26   1–3
- ❏ 27   4–7
- ❏ 28   8–10

Job

- ❏ 29   1–4
- ❏ 30   5–8
- ❏ 31   9–12

June

- ❏ 1   13–16
- ❏ 2   17–20
- ❏ 3   21–24
- ❏ 4   25–30
- ❏ 5   31–34
- ❏ 6   35–38
- ❏ 7   39–42

Psalms

- ❏ 8   1–8
- ❏ 9   9–17
- ❏ 10   18–21
- ❏ 11   22–28
- ❏ 12   29–34
- ❏ 13   35–39
- ❏ 14   40–44
- ❏ 15   45–50
- ❏ 16   51–56
- ❏ 17   57–63
- ❏ 18   64–69
- ❏ 19   70–74
- ❏ 20   75–78
- ❏ 21   79–85
- ❏ 22   86–90
- ❏ 23   91–98
- ❏ 24   99–104
- ❏ 25   105–107
- ❏ 26   108–113
- ❏ 27   114–118

❏ 28	119
❏ 29	120–134
❏ 30	135–142

July

❏ 1	143–150

Proverbs

❏ 2	1–3
❏ 3	4–7
❏ 4	8–11
❏ 5	12–15
❏ 6	16–18
❏ 7	19–21
❏ 8	22–24
❏ 9	25–28
❏ 10	29–31

Ecclesiastes

❏ 11	1–4
❏ 12	5–8
❏ 13	9–12

Song of Solomon

❏ 14	1–4
❏ 15	5–8

Isaiah

❏ 16	1–4
❏ 17	5–8
❏ 18	9–12
❏ 19	13–15
❏ 20	16–20
❏ 21	21–24
❏ 22	25–28
❏ 23	29–32
❏ 24	33–36
❏ 25	37–40
❏ 26	41–43

❏ 27	44–46
❏ 28	47–49
❏ 29	50–52
❏ 30	53–56
❏ 31	57–60

August

❏ 1	61–63
❏ 2	64–66

Jeremiah

❏ 3	1–3
❏ 4	4–6
❏ 5	7–9
❏ 6	10–12
❏ 7	13–15
❏ 8	16–19
❏ 9	20–22
❏ 10	23–25
❏ 11	26–29
❏ 12	30–31
❏ 13	32–34
❏ 14	35–37
❏ 15	38–40
❏ 16	41–44
❏ 17	45–48
❏ 18	49–50
❏ 19	51–52

Lamentations

❏ 20	1–2
❏ 21	3–5

Ezekiel

❏ 22	1–4
❏ 23	5–8
❏ 24	9–12
❏ 25	13–15
❏ 26	16–17

❏ 27	18–20
❏ 28	21–23
❏ 29	24–26
❏ 30	27–29
❏ 31	30–31

September

❏ 1	32–33
❏ 2	34–36
❏ 3	37–39
❏ 4	40–42
❏ 5	43–45
❏ 6	46–48

Daniel
❏ 7	1–2
❏ 8	3–4
❏ 9	5–6
❏ 10	7–9
❏ 11	10–12

Hosea
❏ 12	1–4
❏ 13	5–9
❏ 14	10–14

❏ 15 **Joel**

Amos
❏ 16	1–4
❏ 17	5–9

❏ 18 **Obadiah** and **Jonah**

Micah
❏ 19	1–4
❏ 20	5–7

❏ 21 **Nahum**

❑ 22	**Habakkuk**
❑ 23	**Zephaniah**
❑ 24	**Haggai**
	Zechariah
❑ 25	1–4
❑ 26	5–9
❑ 27	10–14
❑ 28	**Malachi**
	Matthew
❑ 29	1–4
❑ 30	5–7

October

❑ 1	8–9
❑ 2	10–11
❑ 3	12–13
❑ 4	14–16
❑ 5	17–18
❑ 6	19–20
❑ 7	21–22
❑ 8	23–24
❑ 9	25–26
❑ 10	27–28
	Mark
❑ 11	1–3
❑ 12	4–5
❑ 13	6–7
❑ 14	8–9
❑ 15	10–11
❑ 16	12–13
❑ 17	14
❑ 18	15–16

Luke

- ❏ 19   1–2
- ❏ 20   3–4
- ❏ 21   5–6
- ❏ 22   7–8
- ❏ 23   9–10
- ❏ 24   11–12
- ❏ 25   13–14
- ❏ 26   15–16
- ❏ 27   17–18
- ❏ 28   19–20
- ❏ 29   21–22
- ❏ 30   23–24

John

- ❏ 31   1–3

November

- ❏ 1   4–5
- ❏ 2   6–7
- ❏ 3   8–9
- ❏ 4   10–11
- ❏ 5   12–13
- ❏ 6   14–16
- ❏ 7   17–19
- ❏ 8   20–21

Acts

- ❏ 9   1–3
- ❏ 10   4–5
- ❏ 11   6–7
- ❏ 12   8–9
- ❏ 13   10–11
- ❏ 14   12–13
- ❏ 15   14–15
- ❏ 16   16–17
- ❏ 17   18–19
- ❏ 18   20–21
- ❏ 19   22–23
- ❏ 20   24–26

❏ 21	27–28

Romans

❏ 22	1–3
❏ 23	4–6
❏ 24	7–9
❏ 25	10–12
❏ 26	13–14
❏ 27	15–16

1 Corinthians

❏ 28	1–4
❏ 29	5–7
❏ 30	8–10

December

❏ 1	11–13
❏ 2	14–16

2 Corinthians

❏ 3	1–4
❏ 4	5–9
❏ 5	10–13

Galatians

❏ 6	1–3
❏ 7	4–6

Ephesians

❏ 8	1–3
❏ 9	4–6

❏ 10	**Philippians**
❏ 11	**Colossians**
❏ 12	**1 Thessalonians**
❏ 13	**2 Thessalonians**

❑ 14   **1 Timothy**

❑ 15   **2 Timothy**

❑ 16   **Titus** and **Philemon**

Hebrews
❑ 17   1–4
❑ 18   5–8
❑ 19   9–10
❑ 20   11–13

❑ 21   **James**

❑ 22   **1 Peter**

❑ 23   **2 Peter**

❑ 24   **1 John**

❑ 25   **2, 3 John, Jude**

Revelation
❑ 26   1–3
❑ 27   4–8
❑ 28   9–12
❑ 29   13–16
❑ 30   17–19
❑ 31   20–22

Notes

1. See Exodus 4:10,13-17; 32; Numbers 20:5-10.

2. See Exodus 30:1-10,28; 39:38-39; Malachi 1:7; Numbers 4:11.

3. To learn more about Michael, see Daniel 10:13,21; 12:1; Jude 9; Revelation 12:7. To learn more about the ministry of angels to Jesus, see Matthew 4:11; 28:2; Luke 22:43; Acts 1:10-11.

4. See Genesis 3:24; Exodus 25:18-22; 37:7-9; 2 Chronicles 3:14; 1 Kings 6-7; Ezekiel 1:5-14.

5. Roy B. Zuck, *The Speaker's Quote Book* (Grand Rapids, MI: Kregel Publications, 1997), p. 71.

6. The texts that were to be in the phylacteries were Exodus 13:16, Numbers 15:37-41, Deuteronomy 6:4-9, and Deuteronomy 11:13-21.

7. This festival celebrates the purification of the temple in the time of the Maccabean revolt of 167 B.C. It is held on December 25. It is the only Jewish festival not ordained in the Hebrew Bible.

8. Jim George, *The Bare Bones Bible® Handbook* (Eugene, OR: Harvest House Publishers, 2006), p. 198.

9. *Life Application® Study Bible*, New Living Translation (Wheaton, IL: Tyndale House, 1996), p. 975.

10. Adar-Sheni is the thirteenth month, but it appears only in the Jewish leap year.

11. See Genesis 28:10-22; 31:10-13; 32:22-28; 35:9-13.

12. Taken from Jim George, *The Bare Bones Bible® Bios* (Eugene, OR: Harvest House Publishers, 2008), pp. 169-70.

13. See Genesis 2:24; Exodus 20:14; 1 Timothy 3:2,12; Colossians 3:18-19; Titus 2:4; 1 Corinthians 7:3-4; Ephesians 5:23-32.

14. When Jonah 4:11 mentions 120,000 persons "who cannot discern between their right hand and their left," it is counting young children. Based on that figure, Bible scholars estimate that when adults were included, there were approximately 600,000 people in Nineveh.

15. See Matthew 13:1-23; Luke 19:11-27; Luke 15:11-32; Luke 10:30-37.

16. Letters to the churches include Romans, 1 and 2 Corinthians, Galatians, Ephesians, Philippians, Colossians, and 1 and 2 Thessalonians. Letters to individuals include 1 and 2 Timothy, Titus, and Philemon.

17. See Job 1:6-12; 2:1-7; Zechariah 3:1-2; Matthew 4:1-11; Luke 22:31; 2 Corinthians 11:14; 1 Peter 5:8; Revelation 12:9; 1 John 3:8; Hebrews 2:14; James 4:7.

Other Books by Jim George

The Bare Bones Bible® Handbook

The perfect resource for a fast and friendly overview of every book of the Bible. Includes the grand theme and main points of each book, the key men and women of God and what you can learn from them, the major events in Bible history, and personal applications for spiritual growth and daily living.

The Bare Bones Bible® Bios

The lessons you can learn from the outstanding men and women of the Bible are powerfully relevant for today. As you review their lives through the biographical sketches in this book, you'll discover special qualities worth emulating and life lessons for everyday living, which will energize your spiritual growth.

The Bare Bones Bible® Handbook for Teens

Based on the bestselling *Bare Bones Bible® Handbook,* this edition includes content and life applications specially written with teens in mind! They will be amazed at how much the Bible has to say about the things that matter most to them—their happiness, friends and family, home and school, and goals for the future. Great for youth group studies!

A Man After God's Own Heart

Many Christian men want to be men after God's own heart… but how do they do this? George shows that a heartfelt desire to practice God's priorities is all that's needed. God's grace does the rest. Includes study guide. This book has appeared on the Evangelical Christian Booksellers Association's bestseller list.

A Husband After God's Own Heart

Husbands will find their marriages growing richer and deeper as they pursue God and discover 12 areas in which they can make a real difference in their relationship with their wife. (This book was a 2005 Gold Medallion Award Finalist.)

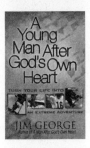

A Young Man After God's Own Heart

Pursuing God really *is* an adventure—a lot like climbing a mountain. There are all kinds of challenges on the way up, but the awesome view at the top is well worth the trip. This book helps teen men to experience the thrill of knowing real success in life—the kind that counts with God. (This book was a 2006 Gold Medallion Award Finalist.)

The Remarkable Prayers of the Bible

Jim looks deeply into prayers of great men and women in the Bible and shares more than a hundred practical applications that can help shape your life and prayers. A separate *Growth and Study Guide* is also available.

A Little Boy After God's Own Heart

(*coauthored with Elizabeth George*)
With delightful artwork by Judy Luenebrink, this book encourages young boys in the virtues of patience, goodness, faithfulness, sharing, and more. Written to help boys discover how special they are, these rhymes present wisdom and character traits for life.

God Loves His Precious Children
(*coauthored with Elizabeth George*)
Jim and Elizabeth George share the comfort and assurance of Psalm 23 with young children. Engaging watercolor scenes and delightful rhymes bring the truths and promises of each verse to life.

God's Wisdom for Little Boys
(*coauthored with Elizabeth George*)
The wonderful teachings of Proverbs come to life for boys. Memorable rhymes play alongside colorful paintings for an exciting presentation of truths to live by.

About the Author

Jim George is a teacher and speaker and the author of numerous books, including *A Man After God's Own Heart* and *The Bare Bones Bible® Handbook.* To order any of his books, email Jim at:

www.JimGeorge.com

Jim and Elizabeth George Ministries
P.O. Box 2879
Belfair, WA 98528
1-800-542-4611